TRANSFORMING

TRANSFORMING THE WORLD?
THE SOCIAL IMPACT OF
BRITISH EVANGELICALISM

David Smith

paternoster press

First published 1998 by Paternoster Press

04 03 02 01 00 99 98   7 6 5 4 3 2 1

Paternoster Press is an imprint of Paternoster Publishing,
P.O. Box 300, Carlisle, Cumbria, CA3 0QS, U.K.
http://www.paternoster-publishing.com

British Library Cataloguing in Publication Data

A catalogue record for this book is available from the British Library.

ISBN 0 85364 819 0

This book is printed using Suffolk New Book Paper which is 100% acid free.

Cover design by Mainstream, Lancaster
Typeset by WestKey Ltd, Falmouth, Cornwall
Printed in Great Britain by Clays Ltd., Bungay, Suffolk

This book is dedicated to the
staff and students of
Northumbria Bible College,
1990–1998. With profound
gratitude for all we have
shared together.

Contents

Preface

Today within the church (we have) many theologically concerned
Christians who have never had a serious thought about transforming
the world, and a goodly number who want to transform the world,
but – disenchanted with traditionalism and fundamentalism – know
no theology.

W. Fred Graham (1978,214)

The quotation above is taken from a fascinating study of the
socio-economic impact of the teaching of John Calvin entitled
The Constructive Revolutionary. I had already decided on the
title of the present book before discovering Graham's use of
the phrase 'transforming the world'. Another Reformed
scholar uses the phrase *world-formative* religion to describe
early Calvinism. The teaching of Calvin, he says, represented
'a fundamental alteration in Christian sensibility' in which the
medieval tendency to turn away from the social world in order
to seek closer union with God was replaced by 'the vision and
practice of working *to reform the social world in obedience to God*'
(Wolterstorff:1983,11. Emphasis mine).

I wish to argue in this work that the Evangelical movement
emerging from the eighteenth-century revival in Britain was a
form of what I will call world-transformative Christianity.
While the individual experience of conversion and the blessing
of personal fellowship with God resulting from it were central
themes in the Evangelical message, these were *not* regarded as
providing an escape from social responsibility. As Chapter 1
shows, many of the early leaders of Evangelicalism were professed Calvinists who traced their spiritual roots back to the
Reformation, via English Puritanism. Consequently, they

inherited a Reformed doctrine of the Christian calling in the world and anticipated that the spread of the Gospel would have significant social consequences – it would 'transform the world'. Although John Wesley and his followers rejected Calvinism as a creed, they were nonetheless greatly influenced by the Reformation and Wesley's teaching on the subject of Christian holiness was intended to 'keep the concept of God-centred behaviour alive in a society which was already beginning to find new bases for action in the market economy, the bourgeois ethic and the modern state' (Kent:1980,477).

Most of the early Evangelicals held a postmillennial view of biblical prophecy which greatly strengthened their convictions concerning the social impact of the spread of the Gospel. Their expectation of the dawn of an age of millennial blessing prior to the return of Christ enabled them to interpret the massive socio-cultural changes occurring during the second half of the eighteenth century in a strikingly positive manner. These changes were 'signs of the times' and harbingers of an age of global peace and justice unlike anything seen before in human history. The extent to which such an expectation became a natural expression of Evangelical spirituality is exemplified in words uttered by the Baptist missionary William Ward. Travelling to India at the end of the century, he looks at the American sailors on a ship drawn up alongside his vessel and cries to God: 'Oh when shall the whole human race have one heart, and that be filled with the love of Christ?'.

The reader will have noticed, however, that the title of this book includes a question mark. *Did* Evangelicalism transform the social world? Indeed, was the vision of the Gospel as a power divinely intended to bring about social transformation maintained, or did the movement abandon this hope and regress to become a new form of other-worldly religion? Chapters 2 and 3 attempt to answer these questions by surveying developments within the Evangelical movement during the nineteenth century. This was the period which witnessed the growth of what has come to be known as 'modernity'. The expansion of Evangelicalism exactly paralleled the explosions of industrialism and urbanization and occurred alongside the spread of quite new ways of seeing the world and the place of human beings within it. Given this changing cultural context, the significance of the question mark in the title of this book is clear: did Evangelicalism transform *this* cultural world, or was the movement itself changed under the impact of modernity?

The question raised here with regard to Evangelicalism is precisely the issue which has been a central concern within sociology in respect of religion in general. The majority of sociologists have concluded that under the conditions created by modern, industrialized cultures the social significance of religion has been eroded. Classical theorists like Max Weber and Émile Durkheim detected changes occurring in religious consciousness in the wake of the social transformations of the modern world which raised questions of critical importance for the future of humankind. The environment of modernity, including the scientific method, the spirit of rational calculation required for the efficient running of a capitalist economy, and what became known as the bureaucratic mentality, created an atmosphere which choked the life from socially significant religion. Very large numbers of people might affirm strong religious beliefs, but such views were increasingly confined to the sphere of private life and ceased to play a formative role in relation to modern culture. In contrast to an earlier generation of rationalist philosophers, Max Weber expressed a deep sense of foreboding about these trends and predicted that modern people would find themselves existing in an 'iron cage' of bureaucracy and rationality. In a famous passage he confessed that he was uncertain whether, when modernity had run its course, new prophets might appear or there might yet be 'a great rebirth of old ideas and ideals'. In the absence of such a rebirth of religious idealism, Weber feared that the future was dark and Western culture would be doomed to 'mechanized petrification, embellished with a sort of convulsive self-importance' (Weber:1985,182).

Sociological theories of religion and secularization have been further developed and refined in the light of fresh empirical evidence in the course of the twentieth century. Yet Weber's analysis of the ambivalent role of modern religion remains relevant and challenging. There is clear evidence that religion has not merely survived under the conditions of modernity but has actually *revived*. Yet the question remains whether such expansion offers any real challenge to the world-view which dominates the modern West? Bryan Wilson, a sociologist of religion working in the Weberian tradition, has no doubt about the answer to this question. Modern religion shows no sign of being able to challenge the dominant ethos of a rationalized, technocratic society. On the contrary, it is increasingly shaped by that ethos, accepting its role in a frag-mented culture by providing an enclave of meaning and sig-nificance to individuals, enabling them to function more efficiently in the everyday world of machines, managers and bureaucrats. Wilson's detailed studies of new religious move-ments leaves him convinced that they 'are not so much the progenitors of a counter-culture, as random anti-cultural assertions' (Wilson:1976,110).

I believe that sociological analyses of this kind raise very serious questions for Evangelicals. Chapter 2 of this book shows how the movement fragmented in the early nineteenth century, while Chapter 3 outlines some of the ways in which Evangelicalism reacted to the challenges posed by the rise of modern culture. It seems clear that the world-transformative tradition of the first generation suffered eclipse during the second half of the nineteenth century. Yet if this evidence seems to confirm the sociological analysis of modern religion outlined above, it must also be noted that there were signifi-cant voices recalling the original vision and insisting that Evangelicals were called to a mission that involved counter-cultural subversion in the context of the modern world. These voices, some of which have been strangely neglected in studies of nineteenth-century Evangelicalism, still speak with rele-vance and power and may yet constitute a significant resource for mission today.

In Chapters 4 and 5 I have discussed more recent develop-ments and consider the challenges facing the Evangelical movement at the present time. Perhaps the key question here is whether the resurgence of the movement during the second half of the twentieth century provides a basis from which it can contribute creatively to the task of Christian mission in the third millennium. This question is made the more urgent by the growing evidence of crisis *within* the culture of the West. Weber's prophetic vision of the loss of human dignity and freedom in a culture operating without a transcendent source of meaning and values has come to pass. Consequently, sociological concern has moved away from a focus on the decline of religion in the modern world, to one concerned with the growing crisis of modernity itself. Even before the term 'postmodernity' came into vogue, an American sociologist who once predicted the demise of religion in a secular culture wrote of the 'poverty' of modernity. The most obvious fact about the contemporary world, he said, 'is not so much its secularity, but rather its great hunger for redemption and transcendence' (Berger:1977,184).

Quite obviously this presents Christianity in the western world with a unique opportunity for renewal in mission. However, the jury is still out on whether Evangelicals in Europe and North America can recover the world-transformative vision of the founders of this tradition and so play their part in the development of a truly critical and missionary engagement with western culture. As I make clear in Chapter 4, the Lausanne Congress of 1974 was a watershed event which offered positive indicators in this regard. Yet Lausanne represented the beginning of a process not the end of a journey and many western Evangelicals have been unwilling to continue up this hard and steep path. The soft options of a fearful retreat to an irrelevant fundamentalism, or an easy triumphalism which mistakes technologically-induced numerical growth for genuine discipleship continue to prove attractive and result in churches which, even if outwardly prosperous, remain enmeshed in the culture of late modernity. Thus, it remains to be seen whether Evangelicalism can return to its roots and become 'an element of criticism and a term of comparison with respect to a society which . . . ceases to be capable of value-judgements and self-criticism' (Aquaviva:1979,194). It is my hope that, in so far as it reminds Evangelicals of the authentic missionary character of their tradition, this book will help toward that end.

Blaise Pascal is reported to have said that authors who say 'My book' should really say 'Our book' because there 'is usually more of other people's property in it than their own'.

The list of people who have helped me along the way with this work is very large and I am grateful to them all. Special mention must be made of Professors Andrew Walls and James Thrower whose teaching and encouragement during my years in Aberdeen were crucially important; of my friends Michael and Elizabeth Middleton who, over many years, have expanded my understanding of the word 'fellowship'; and of Jenny Taylor, whose critical insight and constant encouragement have gone far beyond the normal tasks of an editor. Above all, to Joyce, Andrew and Philip, whose lives have been linked to this work at many levels, I express my loving thanks; in the very deepest sense this is 'our book'. Unfortunately Pascal's statement cannot be stretched to cover the mistakes and errors that remain in this work; for them I alone must bear responsibility.

1

In the Beginning: Evangelicalism as a World-Transformative Religion

Defining words like 'Evangelical' and 'Evangelicalism' has never been easy. Some historians have argued for a very narrow use of this terminology which would restrict its application to a party within the Church of England. In recent times other scholars have treated these words as though they were synonymous with a category which carries deeply negative significance in the late twentieth century – 'Fundamentalist'. The title given to this chapter already suggests that I find such approaches unhelpful, believing that a broader perspective is likely to prove fruitful in advancing our understanding of the Evangelical movement.

What is meant by 'world-transformative' religion will become clear in the pages that follow. However, since this point is central to the argument I wish to pursue throughout the book, it may be helpful to offer some comment here. The relationship between religion and the world is complex and diverse. By definition, religious experience involves claims concerning the reality of the transcendent, a realm above and beyond the world known to the senses. Classical Evangelicalism is profoundly religious in that personal experience of transcendent reality, in the form of individual conversion, lies close to its heart. The crucial question here is whether such experience leads to a devaluing of this world, a turning away from mundane concerns and a preoccupation with a reality perceived to lie beyond time and space. Or does it, in fact, provide believers with a critical perspective on life here and now, enabling them to work for human betterment and social transformation? For Karl Marx and many other modern critics, the answer to the question is clear; Evangelicalism, like all religion, distorts and mystifies reality, offering false comfort to the suffering and providing ideological support to the powerful.

My thesis, simply stated, is that classical Evangelicalism must be declared innocent of this charge. I want to argue that the Evangelical movement which emerged from the 'Great Awakening' in the eighteenth century constitutes a remarkable example of religion as a powerful agent for political and social change; it was *world-transformative*. Prophetically, pastorally and practically key figures provided the necessary corrective to the worst intellectual and social excesses of the age, and again and again acted as the catalysts of reform. This claim embraces not only the history of Evangelicalism within the United Kingdom (with which I am chiefly concerned here) but, through the agency of the missionary movement, its impact on peoples and societies around the world. However, please note the use of the word *classical* here; I am far from arguing that the vision of global, social transformation through the spread of the message of the Gospel, which clearly motivated and inspired the first generation of Evangelicals, was maintained throughout the history of the movement. On the contrary, Evangelicals frequently lost sight of this vision, treated conversion as a means of escape from the present, and adopted attitudes toward social and political tasks which would have baffled Jonathan Edwards or William Carey. Worse still, Evangelicalism gone to seed and providing a religious and theological justification for the growth of market capitalism seemed to provide convincing evidence in support of humanist criticisms of religion. In other words, the story of this movement contains light and shade, highs and lows, resurgence and decline. My hope is that as modern Evangelicals face up to the new challenges posed by the advent of the third millennium, these chapters will help them to recall their origins and measure their claim to this title against the record of the noble men and women who initiated this remarkable tradition.

Roots: Evangelicalism and the Protestant Reformation

While, as we shall see, modern Evangelicalism owes its immediate origin to the eighteenth-century Revival, it is also related to older traditions reaching back to English Puritanism and to the Protestant Reformation. In the fourteenth century John Wyclif was called the 'evangelical doctor' and at his death in 1384 was working on a book with the title *Opus Evangelicum*. Luther and Calvin were both aware of this tradition and in accepting the designation *evangelici* (gospel men) they followed Wyclif by insisting on the supremacy of the Gospel within the Church against the *pontifici* who retained allegiance to the pope. In England Wyclif was given the status of the John the Baptist of the Reformation by the place accorded to him in John Foxe's *Book of Martyrs*.

The links between eighteenth-century Evangelicalism and the Reformation tradition are clearly illustrated in the role played by Martin Luther's writings in the conversion of John and Charles Wesley. Charles discovered the reformer's commentary on Paul's Letter to the Galatians in May, 1738 and records that he spent 'hours in private with Martin Luther'. Some weeks later John Wesley's heart was 'strangely warmed' as Luther's commentary on Romans was read to a meeting in Aldersgate Street. What the Wesleys discovered in Luther was not merely a doctrine of salvation (John was later to have serious doubts about the reformer's formulation of justification by faith alone), but his emphasis upon the personal and experiential character of religion. Important though correct doctrinal definitions might be, what mattered supremely was interior, heart-awareness of Christ's salvation rather than mere intellectual assent to truth. Charles Wesley says that after reading Luther he 'laboured, waited, and prayed' to *feel* within himself what Paul evidently felt when he wrote of Christ 'who loved *me* and gave himself for *me*'. However much the Wesleys might later wish to modify Lutheran teaching there is little doubt that they agreed with the reformer's dictum that the whole of religion can be expressed in terms of personal pronouns.

The importance of the experiential dimension of religion is equally clear in the case of the other great leader of the Revival,

George Whitefield. In this case the literary link with the Protestant tradition was formed by a slim volume from the
previous century which was destined to have a quite extraordinary impact, Henry Scougal's *The Life of God in the Soul of Man*
(1677). Scougal was Professor of Divinity in Aberdeen from
1674 until his early death in 1677. His book, which began life
as a letter to a friend who enquired of him concerning the
essence of true religion, is a classic of Protestant mystical
theology. From these pages Whitefield learned that 'true religion is a union of the soul with God, and Christ formed within
us'. Throughout his subsequent career as an evangelist Whitefield's favourite theme was that of the 'New Birth'; over and
over again as he itinerated across Britain and America he took
his text from Jesus' words, 'Ye must be born again'.

From the first therefore, Evangelicalism stressed personal
conversion. The locus of biblical religion was believed to lie in
the heart of man rather than in his intellect. The central
message of the Revival was in stark contrast to the 'cool and
reasonable theology of the Enlightenment' whose Supreme
Being was remote from human experience. Against this background Evangelicalism insisted on the *immediacy* of God
through a Saviour directly and personally knowable and it
'brought the third person of the Trinity back into common
circulation' (Best:1970,39).

While the experience of the famous members of the Oxford
'Holy Club' was of great significance to the emergence of
Evangelicalism, elsewhere, in parts of Britain as remote as
Cornwall and Yorkshire, similar conversions were occurring
quite independently of the Wesleys. Indeed, few of the early
Anglican Evangelicals owed any direct inspiration to the
Methodist movement as such. George Thompson, who has
been identified as the 'father of the Church Evangelicals',
experienced conversion at least five years in advance of the
Wesleys in the parish of St Gennys in Cornwall (Wood:
1960,133). Charles Smyth conjectured that 'the continuity of
Evangelical doctrine and piety in the Church of England had
never been entirely broken' and he notes that the Bishops of
London and Bristol can be found pleading for Evangelical
preaching as early as the 1720s (Smyth:1943,173). The Revival

was thus a widespread phenomenon in which people scattered across England and Wales recovered emphases on the authority of Scripture, the fallen nature of humankind, the nature of faith and, above all, the need of conversion, which had been abandoned by the theologians of the Age of Reason.

The cultural context

The eighteenth-century Evangelical Awakening occurred at a point in European history when the massive social and cultural changes which marked the dawn of the modern age were accelerating. This period witnessed the growth of the power and prestige of modern science, the rise of industrialism and the painful social dislocations associated with urbanization. This was a revolutionary period in almost every sense of that word and it is important to reflect on the nature of the relationship between the Evangelical Awakening and the Enlightenment. Evangelicalism has sometimes been seen as a reaction to the aridity of Rationalism and Deism. One historian talks of 'mass revivalism of hysterical intensity, in which men and women could find a welcome release from the stresses of a society which provided no equivalent outlets for mass emotion'. The early Methodists have been accused of being anti-intellectual and philistine: there was 'nothing intellectual about Methodism; the rational attitude . . . was absolutely absent'. Such scholars point out John Wesley's belief in witches and in the existence of the Devil, and his magical use of the Bible to obtain divine guidance as evidence that the evangelist's 'superstitions were those of his uneducated audiences' (Plumb:1963,95–6). This is a strange charge against a man who was for ten years an Oxford don with a reputation as an omnivorous reader. Wesley is known to have read Milton, Spenser, Cowley, Waller, Herbert and, even more significantly, Halley on magnetism and gravity, Boyle on chemistry and Drake and Le Clerc's *History of Physic*. Moreover, he retained a lifelong interest in the progress of science, praised Lord Bacon and advocated the empirical approach in the study of phenomena. As Andrews says, 'The Age of Reason never

quite lost its taste for the irrational, while Wesley himself
managed to combine a belief in witches with an interest in
electricity' (Andrews:1969,28).

While Evangelicalism was essentially a 'religion of the heart',
it cannot be understood merely as a reaction to the Enlightenment. For John Wesley the religion of the heart was also the
religion of experience. Knowledge of one's new birth was not
contrary to reason but, although involving an appeal to evidence excluded from consideration by rationalist philosophers,
was confirmed by empirical evidence. Toward the close of his
life Wesley pointed to the visible fruits of his ministry as empirical evidence of the existence and power of God. He claimed that
the Revival, like the events following the Day of Pentecost,
constituted evidence for the truth of the Gospel which any
reasonable person should acknowledge. 'Wesley's ties with the
liberal Enlightenment were substantial' (Semmel:1974,87).

What was true of Wesley and Methodism was also the case
with respect to the wider Evangelical movement. W.R. Ward
argues that Evangelicals shared some of the assumptions of
the Enlightenment and 'constituted the second channel of its
influence'. In particular, they were suspicious of dogma and
endeavoured to apply 'the inductive method in the field of
religion while polemical backwoodsmen were sacrificing truth
to system' (Ward:1972,17). Support for this claim is to be found
in the early issues of the *Evangelical Magazine*. Articles on
religious subjects appear alongside regular features on 'Christian Philosophy' which describe the latest scientific discoveries
in considerable detail. There are explicit calls for the employ-
ment of the empirical method in theological disputes and it is
argued that controversies threatening to split Evangelicals,
like that between Calvinists and Arminians, were the result of
men allowing themselves to be led into a 'metaphysical laby-
rinth'. Such divisions could be avoided if,

> with respect to the abstruse doctrines of scripture, theologians shall
> follow the same method which philosophers have learnt to do with
> respect to the mysterious phenomena in nature: When they shall
> admit them as ultimate facts, and be willing to confess ignorance,
> rather than by attempting explanations to exhibit them in a light no
> less ridiculous than improper.

Evangelical writers often discussed the relationship between Christianity and philosophy and asserted that 'reason is in perfect harmony with revelation and is its admirer and follower'. Faith is not 'in the smallest degree injurious to the principles of real and sound philosophy' and 'the greatest philosopher, if true to his principles, must be the greatest Christian also'. Thus, the journal which was the mouthpiece of the broad Evangelicalism emerging from the Revival reflects Enlightenment principles and advocates empiricism as the only possible approach to serious theology.

In terms of its methodology, Evangelicalism adopted radically new means of evangelism in order to get to grips with social realities in eighteenth-century Britain. Theoretically the *Corpus Christianum* structured religious thought and ecclesiastical practice. However, Evangelicals knew perfectly well that the reality was quite different and their awareness that increasing numbers of people were untouched by the parish system led them to adopt new patterns of itinerant evangelism. This involved, as Gilbert notes, the emergence of *de facto* voluntarism. As early as 1744 Wesley realized that the emerging revival confronted the Established Church with a challenge it could only accept 'by adopting extensive structural and religious-cultural changes'. Anglicanism could either cling to the fiction of the *Corpus Christianum* and turn a blind eye to indications of a growing pluralism in British society, or it could follow the lead given by the evangelists, recognize that its days as a monopolistic religious institution were numbered, and take steps to face the challenge of mission in a changing culture (Gilbert:1976,18–19).

John Wesley's own difficulties in accepting the revolutionary tactic of field preaching illustrate the dilemma facing traditional Tory Anglicans: 'I could scarce reconcile myself . . . to this strange way of preaching, having all my life (till very lately) been so tenacious of every point relating to decency and order, that I should have thought the saving of souls almost a sin if it had not been done in a church' (Dallimore: 1970,274). Yet Whitefield's pioneering ministry among the colliers of Bristol provided irrefutable evidence both of the irrelevance of traditional ecclesiastical structures to the needs

of large sectors of the population and the amazing response
of those same people when the Gospel was presented to them
where they were. Whitefield describes how the colliers were
glad to learn of 'a Jesus who was the friend of publicans and
sinners' and he tells of the 'white gutters made by their tears
which plentifully fell down their black cheeks, as they came
out of their coal pits'. Before long Wesley, aware of the
ignominy he would incur in consequence of the decision,
followed his friend into the fields and commenced a ministry
in which the real and observed needs of people took priority
over the restrictions of an ideal concept of the church which
he now perceived as archaic and unworkable. Wesley's ad-
vice to his preachers, 'go always, not only to those that need
you, but to those that need you most', meant that the main
thrust of the Revival occurred among the classes most alienated from an Established Church increasingly identified with
an unjust status quo. The preaching of the evangelists (including those parish ministers who engaged in 'irregular' itiner-
acy) was a response to the discovery of the clamant needs of
multitudes of people at a juncture in history when the transition from traditional patterns of life to modernity was well
underway and resulting in painful economic and social dislocations. The Revival was thus an essentially proletarian
movement which brought a message of hope to masses of
people to whom the world appeared to be falling apart. It was
in mining districts like Kingswood in Bristol, and in manufacturing towns and villages in the north and west which
were inundated with refugees driven from the land by enclosures, that the preachers discovered undreamt of needs and
reaped an immense harvest. Thus, 'a religious awakening
appeared, district by district, to accompany industrial
growth' (Semmel:1974,9).

Many Anglican incumbents who shared the concerns of
Wesley and Whitefield for the unreached and recognized that
the times demanded the adoption of innovatory evangelistic
tactics, discovered to their chagrin that while their *message*
elicited the most astonishing response among the shepherdless
masses, their *church* had no such appeal. For example, not long
before his death in 1763, William Grimshaw stood with John

Newton on a hill overlooking the parish of Haworth in York-shire and informed his friend that in addition to the growth in his own congregation, he knew of 'five dissenting congrega-tions of which the ministers, and nearly every one of the members, were first awakened under my ministry' (Murray:1971,124). This pattern was reproduced in many places and not a few Nonconformist churches had their origins in the evangelistic activity of some 'methodistical' eighteenth-century vicar. John Berridge, vicar of Everton, itinerated throughout Bedfordshire and Cambridgeshire and fuelled an upsurge of Dissent in those counties.

Alan Gilbert, who describes the period 1740–1830 as a dis-aster for the Church of England, identifies one major cause of the decline of the Established Church in a period marked by widespread religious revival:

> Upholding the social fabric had been a popular enough function while the seams of the fabric had remained relatively unstrained . . . But as the strains imposed by rapid social change grew, what had once been an integrative role took on an obviously partisan character (Gilbert:1976,77).

The Awakening had a significant impact on the old dissenting denominations which traced their history back into the Puritan era. In the early eighteenth century these churches were in serious, many thought terminal, decline. Between 1700 and 1740 their constituency had been halved and Isaac Watts, Old Dissent's most distinguished leader, was prophesying that English Independents and Presbyterians would soon be known only to historians. Dissent seemed locked into the past and incapable of breaking out of the narrow social base of a disappointed élite. Despite continuing intellectual strength, represented by the writing of Philip Doddridge and the bold innovation of Watts' *Psalms and Hymns*, the fact remained that, prior to 1750, Dissent was largely introverted and demoral-ized. Doddridge recognized the failure of Dissent to reach 'plain people of low education and vulgar taste', the very constituency within which the Revival was occurring.

The second half of the century witnessed a dramatic trans-formation in the fortunes of those sections of Old Dissent, chiefly among the Independents and Baptists, which recognized the need and opportunity among the religiously disenfranchised and, embracing the Evangelical theology of the Revival, reaped an extraordinary harvest. The extent of the change within what became known to historians as 'New Dissent' is seen in the comment of the editor of the newly-founded *Evangelical Magazine* in 1793: 'In the beginning of this century there were few persons of evangelical principles in the kingdom; but now, it is supposed, there are more than three-hundred-thousand Calvinists, and many others, savingly converted to God'.

Despite the reminder of the theological division between Calvinists and Wesleyan Arminians in this statement, the writer is profoundly optimistic and expresses the hope that the Revival has laid the foundation for a new age of growth and ecumenism. Bigotry, he says, 'gradually diminishes, and good men of all denominations, laying aside party distinctions, begin to embrace each other with fraternal affection'. Sadly, the political explosion which had recently occurred in France (which many Evangelicals viewed as furthering the purposes of God and a harbinger of the millennium) had thrown its débris into the atmosphere above Europe and when the fall-out began to settle on Britain it so changed the political and religious landscape as to frustrate these sanguine hopes of Christian unity and the arrival of an era of unprecedented blessing.

The optimism just noted was related to a set of eschatalogical beliefs widely held among the Evangelicals. Iain Murray has traced this eschatology back into the Puritan era and has shown how the optimistic interpretation of prophecy among the Puritans bore fruit in the eighteenth-century Revival and the growth of the missionary movement (Murray:1971). A key figure here was the American, Jonathan Edwards, whose post-millennial theology had a profound impact on British Evangelicals. Edwards' interpretation of the Bible led him to believe that mankind stood on the very brink of the long-promised age of millennial glory and his exposition of this hope created enormous excitement in those who read it. The link between William Carey's famous sermon in Nottingham in 1792 on the theme 'Expect Great Things From God: Attempt Great Things For God' (which is usually seen as marking the beginning of the missionary movement) and the eschatology he had discovered in Edwards is obvious when we note the following passage from the American theologian:

> A time shall come when religion and true Christianity shall in every respect be uppermost in the world . . . A time of wonderful union, and the most universal love, peace and sweet harmony; wherein nations shall 'beat their swords into ploughshares' and God will 'cause wars to cease to the ends of the earth' . . . A time when the whole earth shall be united as one holy city, one heavenly family, men of all nations shall dwell together . . . (Edwards:1834,287–8).

Edwards' exegesis of scripture led him to develop what might be called a 'theology of hope', an exposition of the purposes of God within human history that harmonized with the spirit of the age of Enlightenment. Evangelicals believed that the Christian had a duty to read the signs of the times and these all appeared to point to an era of unprecedented progress in human history. The emergence of the Baconian method in science, the stunning work of Isaac Newton, the discoveries of Captain Cook, and the new liberties which seemed to be presaged in the French Revolution, all of this was given a biblical-theological interpretation and formed the foundation for the great advances of Evangelicalism. The *Evangelical Magazine* could welcome the French Revolution in these words: 'The power of AntiChrist is falling; the spirit of civil and religious liberties is spreading; the day has begun to dawn . . . the dark shades of bigotry and superstition are retiring. Men begin to think for themselves . . . The nations begin to see the folly of submitting their *persons* to *civil* and their *minds* to *religious* tyranny'. In contrast to German pietism, British Evangelicalism in this period 'blended in a fruitful way its spiritual purposes with the humanitarianism of a new age' (Van den Berg:1956,124).

In its earliest phase then, Evangelicalism was marked by great optimism. While it certainly stressed the transcendent and spiritual dimensions of faith, it was profoundly concerned with this world and with the outworking of the purposes of God in history. It was *world-transformative Christianity*. It was also basically a plebeian movement, gathering its harvest of souls beyond the crumbling walls of the *Corpus Christianum* and adopting innovative means to meet the needs of masses of people suffering the terrible disorientation which occurs when an old culture decays and the foundations for life itself are removed.

The second phase

The 1790s saw the beginnings of the routinization of the Evangelical Awakening as second-generation concerns with order, discipline and consolidation came to the fore. Of course, such transitions are slow and, at the time, almost imperceptible. As we have seen, the *Evangelical Magazine* was founded in this period and promoted an optimistic vision of a world about to be radically transformed by the spread of the Gospel. The 1790s thus witnessed *both* the growth of undenominational societies *and* a hardening of denominational divisions. There is something tragic about the fact that at the point at which Evangelical religion was about to be domesticated in the interests of distinctive parties, we discover David Bogue preaching his famous sermon on the 'Funeral of Bigotry' at the founding of the London Missionary Society: 'Behold us here assembled with one accord to attend the funeral of *bigotry*. And may she be buried so deep that not a particle of her dust may ever be thrown up on the face of the earth.' The rejoicing was premature; bigotry was to return in many reincarnations and, although the pan-evangelical spirit would survive into the nineteenth century, Evangelicalism was to be influenced and shaped by the deep divisions now emerging within British society.

The last decade of the eighteenth century saw the passing of most of the leaders of the Revival: John Wesley died in 1791, John Berridge in 1793 and William Romaine in 1794. With Wesley's death, Methodism emerged as an entity formally distinct from the Church of England while Berridge was the last of the 'irregular' Anglicans who pursued extra-parochial ministry along Methodist lines. The feeling of transition is further heightened by the emergence of the Clapham Sect in this period. Henry Thornton bought a house in Clapham in

1792 and invited William Wilberforce to live with him. Meanwhile in Cambridge the ministry of Charles Simeon was beginning to make an impact and so to lay the foundation for an Evangelical party within the Church of England.

Viewed from the standpoint of Anglicans who remained committed to the Establishment principle, it is easy to see why a stress on order and discipline emerged at this time. There was need to bring to an end a situation in which, as Charles Simeon put it, clergymen beat the bush and Dissenters caught the game. Yet the re-establishing of parish discipline and the fusion of Evangelical soteriology with an Anglican ecclesiology must also be seen in relation to events in France. We have already seen how in the 1790s the constituency represented by the *Evangelical Magazine* could applaud the French Revolution. In 1792 David Bogue preached a fervently pro-revolutionary sermon in Salter's Hall in London; William Carey, in a clear reference to events across the Channel, wrote approvingly of the 'spread of civil and religious liberty'; while in Scotland Robert Haldane rejoiced in the experiment being made in France. Later, when news of the horrors associated with the Revolution began to filter through, these opinions were revised. At the same time, Anglicans like Simeon and Wilberforce began to develop the notion that Evangelical religion, purged of its enthusiastic excesses, could provide the British state with a bulwark against revolutionary Jacobinism. Indeed, by the beginning of the nineteenth century the *Evangelical Magazine* itself carried an article entitled 'An Essay on the Way to Restore Peace, Good Order, and Prosperity to the Nations'. The following extract shows that, as Kiernan says, 'Jacobinism, which abolished the Christian calendar in France, helped to establish the Victorian Sabbath in England' (Kiernan:1952,44):

> In any country where religion prevails, the Sabbath and the ordinances of the Lord are regularly observed . . . in any part of the country, where persons of rank, and the body of the people, are regular in the sanctification of the Lord's Day, they place a mutual and uniform confidence in one another; and live together in harmony and good order, and in the reciprocal performances of good offices . . . Without intending it, persons of rank by their profanation of the Sabbath, have most effectively taught many of the people the French principles of infidelity, profanity, and levelling of rights and ranks . . . But when

> they shall return to the regular observance of the Sabbath, men of all
> ranks will soon return to their mutual confidence in each other.

Whatever biblical or theological justification it might have, the
observance of Sunday as a Christian Sabbath was clearly assuming immense *symbolic* significance within Evangelicalism.

The emergence of Anglican Evangelicalism

As we have seen, early Evangelicalism reaped an enormous
spiritual harvest among the poor and disenfranchised; we
must now consider how the movement came to be at home
among the upper classes through the emergence of a self-
conscious Anglican Evangelical party. The role of Charles
Simeon in this development was crucial. Macaulay was of the
opinion that Simeon's authority and influence extended from
Cambridge 'to the remotest corners of England' and that his
real power in the church was 'far greater than that of any
Primate'. Simeon's conversion provides confirmation that the
sources of Anglican Evangelicalism were largely independent of the Methodist movement as such. Arriving in
Cambridge he discovered to his consternation that he would
be required to take communion. Overwhelmed by a sense of
unfitness to receive the sacrament, he turned to the eighteenth-century Anglican divine Thomas Wilson for help. After
three months of agonized searching, Simeon made the discovery that his sins might be laid 'upon the sacred head of
Jesus'. He was thus able to obey the university regulation and,
years later looking back on that first communion, he wrote in
his Bible a memento of 'the Easter week and especially that
Easter Sunday, when my deliverance was complete in 1779'.
The details are significant: Simeon's conversion was a deeply
personal experience; it was related to *Anglican liturgy*; and its
central focus was the *crucified* Christ. Fifty-seven years later
a stone was erected in Holy Trinity Church in memory of the
deceased pastor: it records that, 'Whether as the ground of
his own hopes, or as the subject of all his ministrations',
Charles Simeon 'determined to know nothing but Jesus
Christ and him Crucified'.

Generations of Cambridge undergraduates felt the impact of Simeon's preaching and went out to exercise parish ministries across England in which both the form and content of their pulpit labours reflected those of their mentor. They derived from Simeon a moderate Calvinism which, rooted in the exegesis of the whole Bible, avoided dogmatism and insisted on the centrality of Christ in the life and work of the minister. To his student auditors Simeon

> imparted his conviction that conversion – the conscious choice to enthrone Christ as the master of every phase of life, and to live all life as one responsible to God for every thought, word and deed – was the crucial point in a person's life, and that the clergyman had to strive for such conversions alike in his preaching and in his pastoral ministrations (Zabriskie:1940,115).

Simeonite incumbents are encountered frequently in nineteenth-century literature. Not always do they live up to the high standards of personal piety established in Cambridge; indeed, quite frequently they are assailed as examples of cant and humbug. But at their best they are represented by George Eliot's character Mr Tryan, who chose to live among the poor amid dismal lanes and 'between rows of grimy houses, darkened with hand looms', where black dust filled the air. Mr Tryan, says Eliot, 'had a faith that enabled him to labour – enabled him to give comfort to others' (Eliot:1973,350). And, as one of the characters in 'Janet's Repentance' observes, his religion led him to 'give himself up to doing good amongst the poor; and he thinks of their bodies too, as well as their souls'.

Simeon's ministry was critically important in another way: he began the process by means of which Evangelical religion became respectable within the Church of England. The personal abuse he faced at the start of his ministry in Cambridge reflects the wider context within which people like Sydney Smith were publically branding Wesleyans, Calvinistic Methodists and Evangelicals within the Church of England as 'three classes of fanatics' united in 'one great conspiracy against common sense and rational, orthodox Christianity'. Smith hinted darkly that such enthusiasm bore a sinister likeness to the last 'great eruption' of fanaticism which, a century-and-a-half earlier, had 'destroyed both Church and state with its tremendous force'. In modern terms, Smith was suggesting that 'methodists' of all descriptions constituted a 'Militant Tendency' within the nation and that their spread was a genuine cause for alarm. Post-1789 such scaremongering could hardly fail to stir up resentment toward Evangelicals and it explains why they often encountered violent opposition. By fusing an Evangelical soteriology with unimpeachable loyalty to Anglican discipline, Simeon defused such attacks. Indeed, in conjunction with the parallel developments emanating from the Clapham Sect, he made it possible to believe that the spread of Evangelicalism in its Anglican form might actually guarantee the security and stability of the British State.

One specific incident from Simeon's ministry illustrates both his sense of responsibility for his parish and his breadth of spirit. His moderate Calvinism did not please all his hearers. Some left Holy Trinity to attend the ministry of the high-Calvinist dissenting preacher, John Stittle. This man was himself an example of the game beaten from the bush by an Evangelical clergyman and captured by Dissent. He had been converted in a village close to Cambridge during one of John Berridge's forays into the area. Simeon's reaction to the loss of some of his congregation to this brilliant, eccentric, but very poor, preacher was to send Stittle a quarterly allowance which, he said in an accompanying note, was 'for shepherding my stray sheep' (Gray:1921). The Dissenter is recognized (and treated) as a brother in Christ, while the validity of Dissent is denied: the wanderers remain the responsibility of the parish minister. Simeon thus sees Evangelical religion as the means by which new life may yet be breathed into a moribund *Corpus Christianum*.

If Simeon's major contribution lay in the reform and revitalizing of parish ministries, that of Wilberforce was directed toward a much broader goal: the reform of society. Not that the Clapham Sect wished to change the *structure* of British society. On the contrary, Wilberforce showed little interest in domestic social institutions and repeatedly assisted the administrations of Pitt and Liverpool in enacting highly repressive legislation. He was 'steadily opposed to every serious political effort for the help of the oppressed lower orders' (Brown:1961,112). What was needed was the transformation of individuals, and especially of people in the upper echelons of British society. The upper classes needed to be convinced that Evangelical religion, far from presenting a threat to a hierarchical society, could actually secure the continuance of it. Wilberforce believed that the eighteenth century Revival was good as far as it went but that, given the character of British society at the time, it would eventually be judged a failure unless a way could be found to make 'vital religion' attractive to 'those who count'.

In fairness it must be said that Wilberforce was not alone in raising the pertinent question as to how the evangelical message, which had been so successfully communicated by Wesley and Whitefield among the underprivileged in British society, might now be 'translated' and made relevant within the quite different culture of the upper classes. For example, the Baptist writer John Foster, whose socio-political views were as far different from those of Clapham as could be imagined (he viewed royalty 'and all its gaudy paraphenalia as a sad satire on human nature'), wrote an essay in 1802 with the title 'On Some of the Causes by which Evangelical Religion Has Been Rendered Unacceptable To Persons of Cultivated Tastes'. Foster, no less than Wilberforce, was aware that some of the objections of critics were provoked by the intellectual shallowness of the evangelical message and had to be taken seriously (Foster:1867, 213).

However, the men of Clapham were not just concerned to ensure that the form of the message would not be offensive, its *content* should assure the rich and privileged that they might attain personal salvation in Christ without the slightest hint of a threat to their 'station' in life. The *Practical View* of 1797 offered the following ideological justification of Christianity:

> . . . softening the glare of wealth and moderating the insolence of power, [it] renders the inequalities of the social state less galling to the lower orders, whom she instructs in their turn, to be diligent, humble, patient: reminding them that their more lowly path has been allotted to them by the hand of God (Wilberforce:1797,405).

It had often seemed to the British aristocracy that Methodist preaching was socially revolutionary. The Duchess of

Buckingham was appalled by George Whitefield's sermons which, she said, were 'strongly tinctured with impertinence and disrespect toward superiors, in perpetually endeavouring to level all ranks, and do away with all distinctions'.

Particularly offensive was the fundamental Evangelical conviction concerning the universal sinfulness of humankind: it was monstrous, the Duchess protested, 'to be told that you have a heart as sinful as the common wretches that crawl on the earth'. Wilberforce and his friends attempted to make Evangelicalism palatable to the likes of the Duchess by removing the fear that its doctrines involved *social* levelling; in a revolutionary age they presented Evangelical religion in a form which made it 'an attractive and exemplary model for the concurrence of piety and social position' (Best:1970,44). Thomas Chalmers, who owed his conversion to the reading of the *Practical View*, absolved the 'wealthier orders of society' from all responsibility for the degradation and sufferings of the urban poor. In an address to working-class parishioners in Glasgow at the opening of a new school for their children, he defended the social status quo, with its gross inequalities, on the grounds that 'the structure of human society admits no other arrangement'. Chalmers lavished praise on a social order in which the monarchy was 'borne up by a splendid aristocracy, and a gradation of ranks shelving downwards to the basement of society' (Masterman:1900,167–9). There is symbolic significance in the report that Edmund Burke was reading the *Practical View* on his deathbed in 1797 and said that 'if he lived he should thank Wilberforce for having sent such a book into the world' (Pollock:1977,148).

The depth and sincerity of Wilberforce's personal piety is not in doubt, nor can we question the immense significance of his political activity, including his extraordinary lifelong dedication to the abolition of slavery. Viewed on its own terms, Wilberforce's mission was successful: the Christianity of the *Practical View* had a profound effect on the upper classes and many of the commendable characteristics of those who held power in the Victorian era can be traced back, directly or indirectly, to this source. By 1843 the *Quarterly Review* could report 'a substantial increase in religious feelings which has recently developed itself so extensively and so vigorously amongst the members of the Established Church, and especially in the higher and middle classes'. Yet it is hard to avoid the conclusion that, in the form it took at Clapham, Evangelicalism came perilously close to being a religious ideology in the Marxist sense of that term. If this conclusion is correct it has serious implications in relation to secularization: in its Wilberforcean form Evangelicalism may have achieved the success it sought in renewing the Establishment, but a high price was paid for this if, by identifying the Gospel with an élite culture and a deeply conservative approach to domestic politics, it alienated the growing numbers of people who were now challenging the patriarchal structures of British society and calling for radical social reforms. Without intending it, the movement associated with the Clapham Sect may have been a significant factor in the long-term decline of religion in the United Kingdom.

The changing face of Methodism

The early nineteenth century saw developments among Methodists and Dissenters which paralleled those mentioned above. It was always likely that tensions within Methodism would lead to schism once the charismatic figure of John Wesley had passed from the scene. The deep political conservatism of the Wesleys is well known; they had little sympathy with democracy and repudiated any notion that government was derived from the people. One factor in Wesley's formulation of Evangelical Arminianism was his perception of Calvinism as a potentially revolutionary creed. John Calvin has been described as a 'constructive revolutionary' (Graham:1978) who insisted that reformation must be extended beyond the doors of the church. What went on in the Town Hall, the law courts, in the spheres of education, trade and commerce, all of this was to be judged and governed by principles of justice and truth derived from the Bible. Thus, wherever it became influential Calvinism led to 'a systematic endeavour to mould the life of society as a whole . . .'

(Troeltsch:1931,ii,602). To Wesley the complicity of Calvinism in political upheavals seemed proved by English history and by the fact that the Genevan doctrines were widespread among the rebel colonists in America. Yet, given the social base of Methodism, it was not easy convincing grass-roots members that the liberty promised in the Gospel was of a purely spiritual nature and had no bearing on their plight in society. On one occasion Charles Wesley was horrified to spot members of the Methodist society among a crowd of rioting colliers at Kingswood. He leapt into the mob, removed the erring brothers and marched them off for a two-hour prayer meeting at which they 'begged the Lord to chain the lion and were cautioned against apostasy' (Semmel:1974,77). The deaths of the charismatic first-generation leaders, combined with the massive increase in social tensions in the turbulent years toward the close of the century, created a difficult situation for Methodism in which it was forced to choose between maintaining its identity as an essentially plebeian movement, or striking out in a new direction which would remove from it the stigma of political subversion.

Those who have studied the phenomenon of revivals point out the inevitability of a cooling of religious ardour as such movements become routinized. But in this case we can identify deliberate policy decisions which dramatically altered the ethos and direction of the movement. Revival did not just die out in early nineteenth-century Methodism, it was deliberately suppressed by a leadership which regarded it as involving too high a price with a nervous government breathing down the denominational neck. The ruthlessness with which attempts on the part of class members to relate their faith to political questions were suppressed is illustrated in a letter John Stephens wrote to Jabez Bunting in 1821. Reporting on the state of the Manchester Circuit, Stephens boasts that Methodism stands high among the respectable people who have rented most of the seats in the newly erected chapel. His policy with those who had the temerity to suggest a link between Method-ist doctrine and political radicalism is to 'take them one by one and crush them'. The radical ring-leaders now seldom attend Methodist meetings, 'they are down and we intend to keep

them down' (Briggs & Sellars:1973,51). For Stephens and
Bunting, the time for revival was over; 'denominational drill'
was the order of the day. So pliant did Methodism become that
rumours spread among radical activists in the north of England that the denomination's leaders had 'lent the government
half-a-million of money to buy cannon' to fire on demonstrators. The truth, says Ward, was 'more prosaic', but perhaps
more discreditable: the upper crust were using the argument
that Methodism was saving society from revolution to press
the government for legislation making camp-meetings illegal,
while securing the indoor gatherings of the Wesleyans
(Ward:1972,89–90).

There is an obvious affinity between the views of
Methodism's second-generation leadership concerning the social role of religion and the ideas found on the pages of Wilberforce's *Practical View*. Simeon had recognized possible
convergence between Wesley's Arminianism and his own moderate Calvinism when, talking to the aged evangelist in 1784, he
proposed that 'instead of searching out terms and phrases to be
a ground of contention between us, we will cordially unite in
those things wherein we agree' (Moule:1965,80). By 1812 the
Methodist Conference was effusive in its thanks to Lord Liverpool for the repeal of seventeenth-century legislation against
Dissenters and assured the government that Evangelicalism
'soothes the poor under poverty and distress and, by God's
grace, makes them content under the apparently adverse dis-
pensations of Divine Providence'. Wesleyan leaders boasted *ad
nauseam* of Methodism's loyalty and service to the nation and
argued that the evangelical experience of conversion had prevented violent revolution and made possible the industrial and
economic growth of the country. 'Let any gentleman,' said a
Methodist apologist, 'make a tour through the manufacturing
parts of the nation, and he will find as many chapels as villages,
and crowded with attentive hearers.' What is more, such a
gentleman would discover that 'the commerce of the country
was principally conducted by persons who are attached to
evangelical truth' (Semmel:1974,129). Thus, Methodism rein-
forced an emergent Evangelical party within the Church of
England to assure the authorities that, faced with the twin

threats of revolutionary politics and the strains on society aris-
ing from the socio-economic changes of the times, Evangelicalism, far from posing a threat to national stability, offered a way
to ensure a smooth transition to the era of industrial capitalism.
Sadly, the itinerant ministry of Methodism which had been a
device for retrieving the lost from the highways and hedges
'was now being used as a social regulator in a way ruinous to
the self-respect which had been one of Methodism's greatest
gifts to her many humble sons' (Ward:1972,90).

However, while official Methodism set about establishing
itself as a respectable denomination, there is evidence that, at
grass-roots level, this policy caused considerable tensions. In
1813 Jabez Bunting found his claims concerning the apolitical
nature of Methodism undercut by the news that fourteen
Luddites hanged at York had walked to the scaffold singing
Methodist hymns (McLeod:1984,51). Evidence of the fusion of
popular Evangelicalism with radical politics comes from many
parts of the country. When Britain declared war on revolutionary France, the Public Fast and religious service called for in
February, 1794, provoked a massive counter demonstration in
Sheffield organized by the 'Friends of Peace and Reform'. This
was a huge gathering, remarkable in that it was 'at the same
time politically ultra-radical and wholly religious'. James
Montgomery wrote a hymn for the occasion to be sung to the
Old Hundreth and a passionate sermon was preached in which
the progress of civil and religious liberties were seen as inseparable from the advance of the cause of Christ. The linkage at
this meeting between the controversial issues of political reform and biblical perspectives on justice and freedom were
due to 'the influence of radical religious dissenting opinion'
(Wickham:1957,64). Religious history in nineteenth-century
Britain might have been very different if the axis between the
middle and working classes reflected in this Sheffield meeting
had been maintained.

It is clear that two distinct strands of Evangelicalism were
emerging. The movement was increasingly split between
those who saw religion as providing the cement that could
hold a hierarchical society together and those who believed
that it promised the reform of a socio-political order which

negated biblically grounded aspirations for freedom and justice. On the one side was Jabez Bunting, who could declare
Methodism 'as much opposed to democracy as to sin', on the
other were hundreds of thousands of Methodists forced into
secession who saw their faith not as compensation for an
undesirable social situation, but as providing the inspiration
and dynamic to change it. This was the case with Primitive
Methodism which, as a genuine working-class religious
movement, expressed converts' rejection of the assumption
'that the function of religious groups was to encourage social
obedience'. A witness of the 1844 miners' strike near Durham
noted that in Primitive Methodist prayer meetings, 'Everything that could be collected up in the Bible about slavery and
tyranny, such as Pharaoh's ordering bricks to be made without straw, was urged upon them' (Kent:1978,40). Similarly,
when the Bible was first translated into Gaelic in 1801 and its
message spread throughout the Highlands by a new breed of
itinerant preachers, the effect on crofting communities then
experiencing the deleterious consequences of modernization
was certainly not that produced by a strong dose of opium.
Colonel David Stewart of Garth reflected a widespread anxiety about the political consequences of the spread of Evangelical religion in the Highlands when he complained that
Dissenting preachers active in Perthshire in the 1820s were
prone 'to intermix their spiritual instructions with reflections
on the incapacity and negligence of the clergymen of the
Established Church, and the conduct of the landlords, whom
they compare to the task-masters of Egypt' (Meek:1987,13).
Throughout the nineteenth century there are examples of the
Bible being used in this way and, so interpreted, it provided
Scottish crofters and working-class Dissenters in England
and Wales with a concept of salvation which embraced the
spiritual and the historical.

Evangelicalism has come to be thought of largely in terms
of its Anglican, Simeonite development, so that the radical
strand of Evangelical dissent has been overshadowed by the
more ideological religion of 'those who count'. Yet not only in
cities like London, Sheffield and Glasgow, but in rural areas
experiencing grave cultural crises in the wake of massive

socio-economic changes, the message of the Bible and the evangelical experience of conversion often formed the basis for *resistance* to developments perceived to be fundamentally unjust.

2

The Parting of the Ways:
Evangelicalism Fragmented

The growing tensions within the Evangelical movement noted
in the previous chapter were related to the increasing fragmen-
tation occurring within British society. Jonathan Edwards, it
will be recalled, anticipated the literal fulfilment of millennial
prophecies which foretold the destruction of social and ethnic
barriers between peoples. So great was to be the triumph of the
Gospel that an era of global social harmony, peace and justice
would result. However, instead of Evangelical religion shaping and renewing human society, the early nineteenth century
witnessed a reverse process as the social and economic divisions which accompanied the growth of industrial capitalism
split the movement. The dream of the earlier Evangelicals of a
united advance across the world in the name of Christ faded
as denominationalism gained in strength. The Baptists formed
their Union in 1812 and the Independents followed suit in
1832. The event which most clearly symbolized the demise of
the pan-Evangelicalism represented by the *Evangelical Magazine* was the decision of the London Missionary Society, the
very flagship of non-sectarianism, to modify its famous 'Fundamental Principle' so as to exclude Baptists and Arminians
from membership. Bigotry had made a quick return from the
grave and pan-Evangelicalism was about to drown in a rising
sectarian tide.

Among Anglican Evangelicals tensions were also growing.
David Newsome describes the atmosphere of this period as it
was experienced by churchmen of all parties:

> This was a generation of men living through the greatest industrial
> revolution hitherto experienced in the history of the world, and who
> had just witnessed the most terrifying political cataclysm in France
> and who saw all around them the signs of intellectual ferment, the
> cracking of the very fabric of society, a new and purposeful onslaught
> on hallowed institutions (Newsome:1966,55).

John Henry Newman's well-known hymn, 'Lead kindly light,
amid the *encircling gloom*', expressed the feelings of many in
the troubled decades following the Napoleonic wars. Not long
after, the Evangelical H.F. Lyte evoked exactly the same mood
with his 'Abide with me, fast falls the eventide/ The *darkness
deepens*, Lord with me abide'. The feeling, as Lyte put it, that
'change and decay' were evident on every side was heightened
for Anglican Evangelicals by the passing of the leaders of the
movement's 'golden age' and their replacement by men who
lacked the grace and breadth of vision of Simeon and John
Newton.

The emergence of a brash, more doctrinaire type of Evangelical was evident before Simeon's death in 1836 and was typified
by a new journal, *The Record*, which was ultra-conservative and
fanatically anti-papist. The aged Simeon looked on with alarm
and lamented the absence of 'the lowly, subdued humility and
tenderness of spirit' in the new men. Their approach to truth, he
said, showed far too much of the 'dogmatizing spirit' and was
'greatly against the genuine spirit of Christianity' (Jay:1983,
34–5). The new men not only insisted on an increasingly rigid
definition of doctrine but also required ecclesiastical separation
from Christians who declined to accept the new orthodoxy.

Robert Haldane was one of the leaders of this new group.
He returned from a stay in Europe convinced that the truths
of the Bible were about to be undermined by unbelieving
scholarship and set about strengthening the defences by pro-
ducing a two-volume treatment of the doctrine of Scripture.
Haldane believed that Evangelicalism was dangerously vul-
nerable to German-inspired 'neology' as long as it depended
upon the defective teaching of Philip Doddridge concerning
biblical inspiration. Doddridge's admission of different *de-
grees* of inspiration within Scripture was attacked as 'vain
speculations' and replaced with a dogma of plenary, verbal

inspiration. Inerrancy was now claimed for every part of the Bible 'without one single exception' (Haldane:1834,i/169). Haldane claimed that if the 'smallest flaw' could be proved to exist within the Bible its entire authority would have been destroyed. He was confident that 'all the light of science, throughout all the ages of the world, has not been able to discover one single error in the Bible' (Ibid:225). The threat posed by the emerging science of geology was dismissed with the claim that while 'the bowels of the earth have been ransacked' in the attempt to discredit Moses as an historian, the resultant 'absurd' theories have all been exploded and 'no progress whatever has been made toward the detection of any mistake . . . in the sacred writers' (Ibid:ii/121).

It is important to note that this type of apologetic, which was later to prove disastrous for Evangelicalism, provoked a storm of protest when it appeared in the 1830s and was regarded as *discontinuous* with the traditions begun by Wesley, Whitefield and Simeon. Yet the 'strident tone and simplistic attitude' of the new men were to become the 'miserable badge of a new and increasingly influential form of evangelicalism' (Rosman: 1978,90).

The growing doctrinal tensions within the Evangelical movement became clear in a bitter controversy within the Bible Society. The Exeter Hall in the Strand was opened in 1831 and became a favourite meeting place for Evangelical societies throughout the nineteenth century. Yet within a few weeks of this symbolic event, the Bible Society meetings held there exploded in a bitter debate sparked off by conservative demands for the imposition of a doctrinal test to guarantee the orthodoxy of members. This controversy revealed the depths of the divisions within Evangelicalism and showed how the evangelistic impulse was being replaced by a desire to 'protect what had already been gained' (Ibid:96).

This same period also witnessed a further erosion of Evangelical confidence in the power of the Gospel to transform human society. Optimistic postmillennialism now gave way to a new eschatology involving a far more apocalyptic view of history. The new Evangelicals were influenced by the brooding sense of crisis which was given vivid expression in the wider culture in Romantic art and literature. Edward Irving, who was a key figure in this period, publicly acknowledged his debt to Coleridge whom he praised as 'more profitable to my faith in orthodox doctrine, to my spiritual understanding of the Word of God, and to my right conception of the Christian Church than any or all of the men with whom I have entertained fellowship or conversation' (Oliphant:1862,i/205). Irving was incapable of viewing the world in the calm, rational manner of a Jonathan Edwards, as the theatre within which the redemptive purposes of Christ were to be increasingly realized and manifested. Rather, there were dark, demonic powers at work in history and if Christ's ultimate triumph were to be assured, then it had better be relocated *outside* this world. Whereas Thomas Chalmers (with whom Irving had begun his ministry as assistant at St John's Church, Glasgow) saw the Second Advent of Christ as 'a doctrine open to discussion', Irving viewed it as 'a closely approaching stupendous event' (Ibid:23).

This new eschatology had far-reaching consequences with respect to Evangelical involvement in society. John Nelson Darby, founder of the Plymouth Brethren, elevated apocalypticism to a fundamental article of faith and, lecturing in Geneva in 1840, poured scorn on the idea that Christians might anticipate 'continued progress of good' in this world. Such hope, he said, is delusive and all that can be expected within history is a 'progress of evil' (Murray:1971,186). The spread of this negative eschatology led many Evangelicals to retreat from broad historical and cultural concerns. Sociopolitical endeavours came to be regarded as useless, if not actually sinful. In the long term, both the new apocalypticism and the more rigid understanding of the nature of biblical inspiration were to have enormous significance when, having crossed the Atlantic, they became central tenets of orthodoxy within American Fundamentalism.

The theological conservatism of the new Evangelicals was frequently accompanied by a militant political conservatism. Francis Close, who had been influenced by Simeon during his studies in Cambridge, showed just how far the new generation of Anglican Evangelicals was moving away from the

undogmatic form of religion characteristic of the early leaders, when he told a meeting of the Church of England Working Men's Association in Cheltenham, 'In my humble opinion
the Bible is Conservative; the Prayer Book is Conservative;
the Liturgy is Conservative; and it is impossible for a minister
to open his mouth without being Conservative' (Scotland:
1986,129). Given such sentiments it is not surprising that
Anglican Evangelicalism now secured an increasing number
of converts among the Tory landlord class; such gentlemen
'found their conservatism undisturbed – or perhaps stiffened
– by their Evangelicalism' (Rennie:1962,127). The schism between this new, militantly Protestant school of thought and
the Evangelicalism of the Clapham Sect became evident when
Robert Grant attempted to introduce a bill in the Commons
in 1830 to remove civil disabilities from British Jews on the
grounds that 'religious distinctives ought not to be allowed
to interfere with matters of civil privilege'. For the new conservatives this was the thin end of a very dangerous-looking
wedge; once allow the admission of unbelievers to the legis-
lative counsels of a Christian nation and what could prevent
the dismantling of the Protestant state? Terrified by the en-
croachment of liberalism and popery, the new conservatives
were 'driven into a mighty struggle in their attempts to retain
the essential lineaments of the confessional state' (Ibid:92).

Not all Evangelicals in this period, however, were happy to
tread the path which led to rigid theological and social conservatism. On the one hand, Edward Irving and his followers
opted for a far more ecstatic, experiential form of religion.
Irving repudiated the argument, used as an apologetic device
for the defence of miracles, that the supernatural phenomena
described in the New Testament were confined to the apostolic
age and were not to be expected in modern times. He came to
regard his Evangelical Presbyterian heritage as paralyzed by
a barren intellectualism which hindered the release of the
spiritual power by which the authenticity of the Christian
religion might be demonstrated in a changing world. Writing
to his wife in 1825, Irving said he abhorred his 'former notions'
and confessed, 'I was an idolater of the understanding and its
clear conceptions; of the spirit, the paralysed, dull, and

benighted spirit, with its mysterious dawnings of infinite and everlasting truth, I was no better than a blasphemer' (Oliphant:1862,i/351). The link with Romanticism is very clear here. The same can be said about Irving's florid preaching (which Chalmers described as, like Italian music, only 'appreciated by connoisseurs'), and his hunger for ritual and beauty in worship. These strands eventually coalesced in the formation of the ill-fated Catholic Apostolic Church, which has been described as an analogue of the Oxford Movement. Irving, like the Tractarians, was 'utterly desperate of mankind's future' and, given the conviction that civilization was cracking apart, the attempt to recapture the original purity, power and order of the apostolic church was natural enough (Butler:1937,111).

On the other hand, the growing social conservatism among Anglicans opened up a chasm between them and their Dissenting brothers. While the Anglicans became fervent supporters of the status quo, there was increasing political militancy on the part of Dissent. Aware of growing numerical strength, Nonconformists were no longer prepared simply to argue for the right to dissent from a commonly recognized Established religion. With increasing regularity they now expressed root-and-branch opposition to the whole notion of an Established Church. As Thomas Binney put it in 1833,

> It is with me a matter of deep, serious and religious conviction that the Established Church is a great national evil; that it is an obstacle to the progress of truth and godliness in the land; and therefore its end is most devoutly to be wished by every lover of God and man (Rennie:1963,157).

In this situation Evangelicals were doomed to engage in a dialogue of the deaf; Established religion was regarded by one group as the great bulwark against chaos, and by the other as the supreme obstacle to the advance of the kingdom of Christ.

The Chartist movement

The first half of the nineteenth century was a formative period in the growth of distinctive working- and middle-class values in Britain. The emerging middle classes were 'busily distancing themselves from everything that seemed rough, uncultured and vulgar', while the working class was becoming 'less ready to accept humiliating social distinctions' (McLeod:1984,59). When such distinctions were granted recognition and given an air of sanctity within the churches this could hardly fail to have the most serious consequences for British religion. As early as 1816, when Methodism appeared to be once again on the floodtide in parts of England, it was reported from York that while 400 poor people had been added to a congregation, this increase had to be balanced against the loss of the chapel respectability which had defected to the Independents. Ward comments that social tension had already passed the point 'at which it could be sublimated in religious revival' (Ward:1972,83). With the increase in class tensions after the Peterloo crisis in 1821 the tendency of both Methodism and Dissent to reflect the ethos and culture of the rising bourgeoisie grew stronger and Evangelical Protestantism was increasingly fused with middle-class values. Thus, while Anglican Evangelicalism appealed to 'those who count' and attracted growing numbers of the aristocracy, Dissenting Evangelicalism offered a 'place to feel at home' to the newly affluent, and the urban working classes were left to conclude that, however much they might be attracted to Jesus, these churches had little to offer them. In the opinion of E.R. Wickham the economic rise of an increasingly religious middle class 'led to a social stratification in which religious and denominational lines ran parallel to economic ones, so that the poor were excluded both socially and religiously; a fact that both hardened the separation of classes . . . and widened the gulf between the churches and the working classes' (Wickham: 1957,215).

Emerging class divisions were illustrated by the Chartist struggle of 1838–42. The Chartist movement expressed working-class demands that the process of social reform, from which the middle classes had already benefited, be extended to meet their cries for justice and equality. The conflict between the Chartists and the established churches has sometimes been treated as a contest between the forces of order and religion, on the one side, and those of infidelity and revolution on the other. Yet, as Eileen Yeo has shown, such a perception of the

period fails to take account of Christianity, 'not as the posses-
sion of any one social group, but as contested territory'
(Yeo:1981,106). The Peterloo massacre had left deep scars on
the memories of the working classes and became a powerful
symbol of the callous disregard of the rich and privileged for
the sufferings of the poor and oppressed. Yet, while some
working people were driven to atheism and secularism as a
result of the massacre, the evidence suggests that their numbers were small and that a more widespread reaction was the
attempt to articulate a counter-Christianity which would 'deliver the religion of Jesus Christ from the disgrace brought
upon it' and ensure its continued credibility with working
people (Ibid:110).

The climax of the Chartist struggles occurred between July
and September of 1839 when working men, wearing their
everyday clothes, attended Sunday worship in parish
churches in at least thirty-one localities across England and
Wales. In most cases only a single demonstration occurred,
as in Stockport on 21 July. Elsewhere parish churches were
reluctant hosts to Chartists for many weeks. In Sheffield they
were present on five consecutive Sundays before being met
at the church gates by armed police on 15 September and
informed that only 'decently dressed individuals' would be
allowed into the service. The demonstrations were invariably
orderly and reverent. Yeo found only one instance of a sermon being heckled when the vicar of St Stephen's, Norwich,
having announced his text from Philippians, 'I have learned,
in whatever station of life, therewith to be content', was
interrupted by the cry, 'You get £200 a year – come and weave
bombazines!' In each case the demonstrations were announced in advance and the Chartists requested a sermon
from a specific text. Their favourite passage (and the one most
often ignored by the preachers) was James 5:1–6, a section
which bears the heading 'Warning to Rich Oppressors' in one
modern translation. Most incumbents responded with lectures on the need for patience, respect and submission to
divinely constituted authorities. In Blackburn the Chartists
actually got a sermon on their chosen passage but, by a
remarkable piece of casuistry, the preacher concluded that

while the Roman rich might fall under James' strictures, so to castigate the modern rich would be gross injustice. Elsewhere the clerical response descended to the level of calculated insult. The vicar of Cheltenham, Francis Close, accused the Chartists of entering the church in 'an unhallowed spirit' and thundered against socialism as 'rebellion against God' and Chartism as 'rebellion against man' (Scotland:1986,129). In Ashton the curate chose as his text, 'My house is a house of prayer but ye have made it a den of thieves'. This was too much for the demonstrators and they immediately left the service. Yeo concludes,

> The clergy could not have played their parts better had they set out to prove the Chartist case that they were wolves in sheep's clothing who legitimized oppression while pretending to speak the word of God. The setting of public confrontation was not one in which the clergy could be expected to extend an olive branch: but they went extravagantly to the opposite extreme, heaping fulsome praise on the existing social order, allowing the Chartists no shred of dignity or vestige of a case (Yeo:1981,134).

The Chartists had entered the churches in an attempt to challenge from within what they perceived to be the perversion of Christianity by the ruling, and rising, classes. Their determination to attend worship wearing working clothes and their deliberate occupation of pews which were set aside for the rich and prosperous, involved the assertion of the value of labour in the sight of God and the absurdity of exclusion on the basis of dress or poverty. Viewed from the other side, working aprons and clogs were an affront to the sense of 'respectability' which, by this time, was equated with godliness, while the occupation of the pews of the rich was 'a gesture of menace toward private property and the disruption of a carefully contrived display of social hierarchy' (Ibid:132).

To many people the confrontation of 1839 seemed to have epochal significance. J.R. Stephens, one of the few clergy active in support of the Chartist cause, warned that Christ was now saying to England, as he once said to the Jews, 'How often would I have gathered you as a nation . . . but ye would not!' God, he said, was giving the country its last opportunity and the Chartist movement represented the eleventh hour of the day of national salvation. Such apocalyptic expectations were not to be realized, but it is difficult to avoid concluding that the credibility of institutional religion in Britain was seriously damaged by the humiliation of the working people who attempted to argue the justice of their case for radical social changes by challenging the interpretation of the Bible and the form of Christianity offered to them by the guardians of orthodoxy.

A prophet without honour

It is important to take note at this point of a forgotten representative of the Evangelical tradition who possessed prophetic insight into the weaknesses of institutional religion in Britain at mid-century. I refer to Edward Miall who, in the year following the great Chartist demonstrations, informed his congregation in Leicester that he was relinquishing the pastorate in order to devote his energies to the founding of a new journal which would become the mouthpiece of a campaign for disestablishment and radical social reforms. After two years soliciting financial support, the first issue of Miall's paper, the *Nonconformist*, appeared on 14 April, 1841. The remarkable thing about Miall was that, while fervently committed to the Dissenting cause, he recognized the extent to which nonconformity had itself become allied to narrow class interests and saw, probably more clearly than any other nineteenth-century Evangelical, the immense damage which such alliances would cause in the long term. Unfortunately, Miall is remembered (if at all) only as a militant opponent of established religion. However, he discerned potentially fatal weaknesses in British Christianity *in toto* and delivered lucid and penetrating critiques of all the churches. Miall was one of the few men to make an active attempt to repair the damage done to the churches by the treatment accorded to the Chartists in 1839. With Sturge, Bright and others, he arranged a series of conferences with Chartist leaders in Birmingham to plan a campaign for the abolition of class-based legislation. In 1844 he founded the 'British Anti-State Church Association', which later changed its name to the more felicitous 'Society for the Liberation of Religion from State Patronage and Control'. This organization became popularly known as the 'Liberation Society', a development that must have pleased Miall since he believed most profoundly that the separation of Church and State would actually effect the liberation *of* religion, setting it free to be itself and to fulfil its proper function. Thus, to Anglican opponents Miall argued that disestablishment was as much in the long-term interests of the Church of England as it was of Dissent; his hostility 'was not to the church but to what he regarded as the fatal incubus of state patronage'.

Miall's book *The British Churches In Relation To The British People* (1849) offers an incisive contemporary analysis of British culture at mid-century. There is, he maintains, a general malaise in the British churches and he sets himself the task of identifying and explaining the causes of this alarming condition. Man, he says, occupies the first place in the attention of Christians, God plays a subordinate role. Contemporary religion has developed a concept of salvation which is utilitarian in character: the salvation which it searches after, receives, exhibits, and enforces, is summed up in three words, the 'greatest possible happiness' (Ibid:138). Religion's demands are restricted to the formal act of public worship so that godliness no longer involves the whole of life, but merely 'a sort of inclosure railed off from the entire surface of existence' (Ibid:141). Miall laments the formal respectability which many of the novelists describe as pervasive in Dissent by this time. To a generation content with the illusion that they lived in a profoundly religious society, Miall sounds a warning: the real influence of the Gospel on those who regularly submit themselves to the ministry of the churches is 'slowly but steadily lessening' (Miall:1849,152).

In the second half of the book Miall turns his attention to the masses outside the churches and, two years before the 1851 Census suddenly jerked the churches into an awareness of social realities, he says that most working men, 'taught to regard the Church Establishment as sanctioning and abetting the oppression which crushes them to the earth', are moving from 'distaste' for the solemnities of religion to a 'malignant hatred' of it. Yet the churches continue to dream of Britain as a Christian nation and so remain ignorant of the extent of 'spiritual destitution concealed behind the screen of baptized nominalism' (Ibid:381f).

The man-centred nature of religion bemoaned by Miall is also reflected in the churches' failure to conform practice and preaching to the ethic of the Gospel. Christianity has capitulated to what he calls the 'aristocratic sentiment' and the 'trade spirit'. By the former is meant assigning value and worth to people according to the external circumstances of their lives. The British churches are riddled with forms of intellectual and cultural snobbery which completely invert the teaching of Christ with regard to the worth of people in the sight of God:

> Religion as embodied in the written word of God, and in that more emphatic living Word which was 'made flesh and dwelt among us', uniformly champions . . . the cause of the weak, the friendless, the oppressed – religion, as embodied in modern organizations, preaches up the rights of the powerful, and dwells mainly on the obligations of the powerless . . . Once her favourite occupation was to move as an angel of mercy among outcasts . . . in our day she is more at home with the comfortable, than with the wretched' (Ibid:203–4).

It is interesting to note Miall's attitude toward the missionary movement. Christian missions had become fashionable and were increasingly identified with the national mission of a 'Christian nation'. The annual May Meetings at the Exeter Hall, to which Evangelicals flocked from all parts of Britain, became the focal point of the movement and, as such, attained great significance for its supporters, while drawing considerable fire from its enemies. For example, in 1844 *Punch* carried an article with the title 'Exeter Hall Pets' in which it contrasted the affection of Evangelicals for the 'benighted sons and daughters of earth thousands and thousands of miles away' with their apparent ignorance of the 'destitution of the alley that abuts upon their dwelling-place'. With some folks, *Punch* asserted, 'sympathy, like Madeira, is all the better for a sea voyage' (*Punch*:1844,210). Miall conceded the point: foreign missions had reached the stage of fashionable patronage and it was a sad fact that many who subscribed liberally to secure the conversion of the heathen at the antipodes, evinced 'little or no compassion for the scarcely less degraded heathen at home' (Miall:1849,206). Perhaps it is not surprising that the Exeter Hall committee, having seen the prospectus for the series of lectures which formed the basis of this book, refused Miall the use of the building for the propagation of his views. Evangelicalism thus closed ears and minds to a prophetic voice which, had it been heeded, might have made a considerable difference to the subsequent history of religion in Britain.

Edward Miall realized that the association between institutional religion and the 'aristocratic sentiment' led to the alienation from the churches of masses of people for whom élite culture was both foreign and, because it was recognized as a badge of those responsible for the oppression of the poor, hated. The great majority of workers, Miall claimed, were already lost to the churches and 'a leaven of bitter infidelity is at work among them'. Anglicans and Dissenters were alike responsible for this since it was their representation of Christianity which 'exiles the most oppressed, the meanest, and the most wretched of our countrymen'. Religious people should not be in the least surprised when the resentment of the manufacturing population led them to 'see in our Christianity a foe to be humbled by any and every means within their reach' (Ibid:221).

But, however serious the fusing of Christianity with the 'aristocratic sentiment' may be, the 'greatest and most pernicious practical error' of the times is the pervasive influence of the 'Trade Spirit' among middle-class Christians. Miall defines this as 'the disposition to pursue trade with an exclusive . . . view to the worldly advantage to be got by it – making it its own end' (Ibid:299). On page after page he indicts the religion of his time for its capitulation before the idols of Mammon and its utter failure to relate the worship of Christ to the practice of commerce. Christian men, he says, seek God in church and totally ignore him in their factories, counting-houses and shops. Miall was forced to the sad conclusion that in the sphere of business there was no essential difference between the Christian and the non-Christian: 'the lust of speculation is as rife in the one as in the other' and religious men had abandoned 'Christ's code of morals in their trade transactions'

(Ibid:307–8). Leading Evangelicals who 'give princely sums' to support overseas mission act in the business realm 'almost exclusively upon the hard, inflexible, inexorable maxims of commercial economy'. The terrible consequences of this failure to relate the ethic of Christ to economic activity were seen most clearly among the wretched of the earth:

> Many a bleeding, pining, broken heart – many a shattered family circle . . . has borne witness before the merciful Ruler of all, against the desolation which has swept their hopes and prospects in consequence of the inconsiderate cupidity of the disciples of Jesus, and their exclusion of his gentleness of spirit, and kindliness of disposition, from all their transactions in secular business (Ibid:324).

The ethical compromises of the churches were directly related to their failure in mission, believed Miall, for, by succumbing to the 'trade spirit', they 'create the impediments which they strive in vain to surmount' (Ibid:341). Miall's emphasis here had much in common with the modern notion of *structural* sin. Sadly his warning to Evangelicals, that their preoccupation with the religious life of the individual was blinding them to issues of fundamental importance with regard to Christian witness in industrialized, urban society, went largely unheeded and as secularization gathered pace in the second half of the century, they clung to the vain hope that a revivalism which viewed political and commercial issues as outside its area of concern might stem the advancing tide of irreligion.

Edward Miall's *The British Churches In Relation To The British People* was important not just as a remarkable piece of social prophecy, but as the first in a series of volumes which kept alive the world-transformative tradition within Evangelicalism. Thomas Guthrie's *The City, Its Sins And Its Sorrows* (1857), Andrew Mearns' very influential *The Bitter Cry of Outcast London* (1883) and, most famous of all, William Booth's *In Darkest England And The Way Out* (1890) all belong to this genre. In all of these works Miall's concern at the concessions made by Christians to the aristocratic sentiment and the trade spirit are repeated, his warnings concerning the alienation of the working classes are re-emphasized, and his call for the recovery of the moral and ethical comprehensiveness of the Evangel is echoed.

Evangelicalism approaching mid-century

As we have seen, Evangelicals were no longer agreed as to what the Gospel might be expected to achieve in this world. Many came to regard the vision of a world in which every aspect of human life on earth would be enriched by the progress of the kingdom of Christ as unbiblical and substituted it with a concern for the maintenance of the purity of a subculture which stood over against the wider world. The Baptist essayist John Foster admitted that some Evangelicals defended their lack of reading with the retort that 'they thought it enough to read the Bible' (Foster:1867,202). By mid-century there was growing evidence of a split between the religious and secular worlds and Elizabeth Jay talks of an identifiable 'Evangelical backlash' against the fine arts (Jay:1979,190). This is typified by Francis Close's militant opposition to horse racing, theatre-going, galas and a host of activities which he included under the rubric of 'vain pleasure'. When Cheltenham's Theatre Royal was destroyed by fire in 1839, Close declared this an 'act of God' and ensured that the place was not rebuilt during his lifetime. Donald Davie sees this period as one in which English Dissent betrayed its intellectual and cultural traditions and capitulated to philistinism (Davie:1978,56). Certainly contemporary critics complained, in the words of Leslie Stephen, that Evangelicalism too often displayed 'a hatred of all that makes the world beautiful, combined with a hearty appreciation of everything that adds to its material comfort' (Ibid:77). In *Middlemarch* George Eliot presents Mrs Bulstrode as an example of the easy juxtaposition of Evangelical religion with affluence when she is described as happily combining 'the nothingness of this life and the desirability of cut glass, the consciousness at once of filthy rags and the best damask' (Eliot:1986,263). Later in the century Gladstone was to observe that while Evangelicalism distanced its adherents from the best literature, art and culture, it seemed to harmonize very well with 'money-getting pursuits' (Gladstone:1879,13).

This same period also witnessed the growing challenge which the new science of geology presented to Evangelical theology. The traditional view that the biblical flood story was supported by empirical evidence of a global catastrophe was widely questioned and many Evangelicals felt the ground shift beneath their feet. There were many devout Christians who were able to accept the new science without the slightest alarm. For example, Hugh Miller and John Fleming, who both followed Thomas Chalmers into secession at the Disruption of the Scottish Church in 1843 and were men of unimpeachable orthodoxy, refused to allow their scientific investigations to be restricted by a particular interpretation of the Bible. Miller, who was a brilliant geologist, said that theologians who opposed his findings on the basis of a literalistic reading of Genesis should reconsider *their* approach to the interpretation of Scripture. Fleming, whose critique of catastrophist geology anticipated Charles Lyall's uniformitarianism, attacked preachers who assumed 'that the first principles of geology were revealed to Moses and communicated in the book of Genesis' (Livingstone:1987,13–14). A contributor to the *Evangelical Magazine* in 1840 noted that 'well meaning but misguided men have taken alarm' and have begun to attack geology 'as the foe of revelation'. The writer will have none of this: what is needed is not an obscurantist flight from the new learning, but a frank recognition that traditional interpretations of the Bible have been 'very erroneous'. Genesis is capable of being harmonized with the best discoveries of modern science and, since 'truth can lose nothing by investigation', Christians must examine the findings of geology 'with the calmness and impartiality which its importance demands'. The author realizes that he is likely to be accused of infidelity for these opinions, but such a response can only come from persons 'who have imbibed much of the spirit that led their predecessors to incarcerate Galileo' and they need to be warned that such intemperate violence 'may greatly injure the cause they wish to serve'.

It was a prophetic warning and it reminds us that, as in the area of socio-political concern, Evangelical Christians responded in different ways to the new situation. If some were inclined to pull up the drawbridge and retreat within the impregnable walls of an inerrant Bible, assured that Scripture closed off all arguments on matters of science and history, others were perfectly willing to go out and meet the supposed enemy, convinced that a battle for the Bible would be a completely phoney war.

By mid-century then, Evangelicalism had ceased to be a homogeneous movement. We might almost speak of a *variety of evangelicalisms*. When the Evangelical Alliance was founded in 1845 it resulted, not from an ecumenical and world-transformative vision like that which had animated an earlier generation of men like David Bogue and Thomas Haweis, but from a fear of resurgent Catholicism. And even this fear was not enough to attract Anglican Evangelicals to the Alliance for, apart from a few men like Edward Bicker-steth, the majority suspected the Alliance of being the Trojan Horse of disestablishment and so 'conquered their sympathy for its aims and refused to touch it' (Chadwick:1966,441). Indeed, the *Christian Observer* made ferocious attacks on the Alliance and castigated Anglicans who were willing to 'fraternize with Anabaptists' (Balleine:1908,254). Thus, Evangelicalism moved into the second half of the nineteenth century ill-equipped to confront the challenge of an era of widespread doubt.

3

Victorian Evangelicalism:
Holding the Fort in an Age of Doubt

The Victorian era for Evangelicals can be said to be largely characterized by attempts to retain their hold on a culture which was increasingly adrift from its Christian moorings. The year 1851 was especially significant. It was the year in which the results of the religious Census, carried out on a fine Sunday at the end of March, confronted Christians of all persuasions with statistics which challenged assumptions that Britain was a profoundly religious nation. The Census, and Horace Mann's commentary on it, revealed that Dissent was now practically equal to Anglicanism in numerical strength, yet both groups were given food for thought by the discovery of their common failure to make an impact on the working classes. Mann himself believed that the most significant finding to emerge from the exercise was the discovery of the alienation of an entire class of people from institutional religion. Whether the cause of working-class irreligion lies in themselves or in the treatment they suffer from the churches, he wrote, 'it is sadly certain that this vast, intelligent and growingly important section of our countrymen is thoroughly estranged from our religious institutions' (Wickham:1957,110).

Lord Shaftesbury recognized that the time had come for drastic reforms of the archaic structures of Anglicanism in order to meet the challenge of the missionary task at home. The Church of England was hamstrung by outdated legislation which prevented Anglican evangelists from adopting innovative methods in order to reach the thousands who, it was now clear, would not attend regular services in a parish church.

Four years after the Census, Shaftesbury introduced the Religious Worship Bill in parliament with a warning that 'Unless the Church is able to act as a missionary Church, and by the removal of every restriction upon her free actions to compete fairly with all other denominations, my belief is that she will be lost . . . very speedily' (Balleine:1908,246). Thus, a century after Wesley and Whitefield had raised the alarm and declared that the structures of the *Corpus Christianum* were an obstacle to evangelization, Shaftesbury recognized the reality of religious pluralism and the imperative need to relearn the art of being 'fishers of men'. Whether the proliferation of mission agencies and evangelistic services in theatres which followed the 1855 Act was an appropriate response to the religious needs of Britain in the second half of the nineteenth century is open to doubt.

By a strange irony, at the very point at which Anglicanism began to modify its stance in the face of the challenge of working-class irreligion, Nonconformists were demonstrating the extent to which their alliance with the bourgeoisie was blinding them to the urgency of the situation. Methodism continued its dismal course of social and political conformism and, following a fresh upsurge of grass-roots democratic passions after 1848, the unbending Toryism of its leaders resulted in the loss of a third of the denomination's membership within five years. In a long review of the Census findings the editor of the *British Quarterly Review* informed the poor that 'it would be an intense gratification to the middle and wealthier classes everywhere, to see their neighbours from a humbler lot assemble with them in their common acts of worship' provided that the 'preliminary for public worship', viz., 'cleanliness', be 'attended to'. It is difficult to imagine a response to the situation uncovered by the Census more heartless and patronizing than this one: the poor are reproved for their ingratitude in absenting themselves from 'free sittings' provided by the middle and upper classes' voluntary contributions and readers are informed that for most working people, 'the great luxury of Sunday is, that they can lounge in their unwashed condition on that day more freely than on any other'. How representative of Evangelical Dissenting opinion this article was is difficult to judge, although Thomas Binney had argued that Congregationalism's special mission was 'neither to the very rich nor to the very poor' but to the great middle section of the community (Inglis:1963,15), and R.W. Dale defended the same denomination's middle-class character on the grounds that it had been called by God to minister to intellectuals.

However, it is important to note that the sprawling cities of Victorian Britain were the breeding ground for an immense variety of new religious groups in this period. This 'religious underground' is often overlooked, yet a contemporary observer noted that offshoots from existing denominations were mushrooming everywhere and that in every large town in England, small groups of devout believers met 'in little upper rooms in the back streets'. He cites an example from Manchester:

> Not bound together by any rigid orthodoxy, and eschewing any sectarian name, they were what would ordinarily be called strongly evangelical...They had no minister...[and disliked] what they called the 'one-man system'. As near as might be they conformed to the habits of the early church...and lived an obscure, but simple, happy, useful religious life (Brooke Herford, in Cunningham:1975,31).

The writer George MacDonald, alienated from Congregationalism by its dogmatic narrowness and social conformism, hired a room in Manchester where he might preach to any who would listen to him unshackled by denominational ties: 'If anyone does not like what I say he can go away and welcome; but not all can turn me away . . . We have no odious ungodly seat-rents and distinctions between rich and poor' (Triggs: 1986,53–4).

Evangelical social concern in Scotland

Thomas Guthrie arrived in Edinburgh in 1837 after a successful ministry in rural Tayside and at once realized the irrelevance of traditional patterns of parish ministry in the face of the appalling problems created by industrialization and urbanization. Guthrie was no romantic, longing for a return to pre-modern social structures; on the contrary, he saw divine providence at work in the growth of cities which he describes as 'the cradles of human liberty'. Yet, while repeatedly thanking God for the cities, he was acutely aware of the terrible sufferings of the poor and warned that religious, social and political disasters loomed over Britain if the plight of the masses was ignored. Guthrie's analysis of working-class irreligion is the antithesis of that found in the *British Quarterly Review*: the pattern of life in the backstreets and alleyways is not something freely chosen by the poor, it is imposed upon them by inherited and inescapable social conditions. As a minister of the Gospel which 'recognizes no distinction between rich and poor', Guthrie protests against the wrongs done to the deprived populations of the cities which 'deserve succour rather than censure' and are 'more to be pitied than punished' (Guthrie:1857,80). The poor, he said, were doubly deprived of justice. On the one hand, they lived in conditions of such squalor and destitution that they were driven to seek food by any means possible; on the other hand, respectable society exacted retribution upon them for crimes which were traceable to its own heartlessness and indifference: 'We first condemn them to crime, and then condemn them to punishment. And where is the justice of that?' (Ibid:98). Guthrie admits that had society treated him as it treated the poor, he would have hated it and sought vengeance upon it. He issues a chilling warning to the upper classes that if they continued to ignore the demands of social justice, there would be a convulsion in which the pyramidal structure of British society would topple over and bury throne and altar in a common ruin:

> The upper classes should know – God grant that they may not learn the lesson when it is too late! – that whatever be the distance between them, no elevation separates their interests from the lowest people; that there is a God who reigneth upon earth; and that by a decree of providence, as sure as those that rule the courses of tide or time, those who neglect the interests of others shall themselves suffer in the end (Ibid:118).

For Guthrie, the teeming masses in London and Glasgow were the 'heralds of death' for Britain and he demanded of all denominations that they devise radically new solutions to the problems of evangelizing the cities. The traditional parish system, which had evolved in quite different social conditions, was an obstacle to urban evangelization. What was needed was for city churches to form 'a real working Evangelical Alliance' so that they might act together in confronting the situation as it existed in 'the dark and destitute districts of the city'. Guthrie proposed that every church-going family should undertake the care of a single family in the slums; this would 'prove a blessing to the families visiting as well as to the families visited' (Ibid:113). If this strikes us as simplistic, at least it was an attempt to throw a bridge across the class divide and to insist that traffic over that bridge must be two-way. Guthrie complains that the upper classes were separated by a huge gulf from the masses and, unlike those who insisted that the poor must adapt to middle-class culture before being admitted to the churches, he places the onus on the privileged. Let *them* undergo the painful process of initiation into the realities of life in the slums.

Guthrie's book challenged Evangelicalism's identification with middle-class culture and argued that working-class irreligion was likely to be increased by the fatal connection which the poor perceived to exist between the churches and the socio-political structures of a society that condemned them and their children to unmitigated suffering.

Guthrie has less to say about the evils of the 'trade spirit' than Miall, but when we find him complaining of 'a system of trade which offers up our children in sacrifice to the Moloch of money and builds fortunes in many instances on the ruins of public morality and domestic happiness' (Ibid:104), we detect the beginnings of an Evangelical critique of unbridled capitalism. The book provided Evangelicals in the city of Glasgow with an approach to social theology which was significantly different from that which they had inherited from Thomas Chalmers. So uncritical was Chalmers' advocacy of *laissez faire* that he argued that if men were released from 'the chain of their own interest', they would be like 'dogs of rapine let loose'. Chalmers claimed that 'selfishness is the grand principle on which the brotherhood of the human race is made to hang together' (Chalmers:1820,76). By the 1860s, when the problems of urban destitution had exposed the inadequacy of such views, Guthrie's book stimulated growing concern about life in the slums and led to a readiness to seek new explanations for the plight of the poor. Evangelicals in Glasgow began to give expression to the belief that 'the single-minded grasping for wealth in the free-market economy was detrimental to the moral, physical and spiritual condition of the working classes' (Brown: C.G.: 1981,433).

Forms of radical Evangelicalism can be traced in Scotland throughout the Victorian era. By mid-century the preaching of itinerant evangelists and successive waves of revival had led to the widespread acceptance of Evangelical religion in the Highlands. At a time when unprecedented social changes were destroying the fabric of traditional Gaelic society and prompting passionate debates on the issue of the ownership of land, resistance to the enclosures and to rural depopulation was largely based on concepts of justice derived from the Gaelic Bible. The membership card of the Highland Land Law Reform Association contained the text, 'The profit of the earth is for all' (Eccl.5:9) followed by the Gaelic motto, *Is treise tuath na tighearna* ('A tenantry is mightier than a lord'). A witness of a meeting of farm servants involved in a rising against their employers in the 1860s reported that 'the bulk of their imagery and appeal was almost entirely from Holy Writ'. The effect of appeals to biblical economic principles was electric: 'excited figures raised to an enthusiasm almost as wild as followed the appeals to liberty, equality and fraternity, made in the cafés of Paris in the time of the Revolution' (Dunbabin: 1974,233).

The Gaelic Bible thus provided the conceptual framework within which generations of Highland preachers were able to interpret historical change and urge popular resistance to developments which were discerned as fundamentally unjust. The texts employed by these preachers, and the hermeneutical method by which they were related to the plight of the Highland people, has led one scholar to describe this as 'A Highland Theology of Liberation' (Meek:n.d.).

The rise of 'modern thought'

As the nineteenth century wore on the issue that loomed large
for Evangelicals was that posed by the growing strength of
what came to be known as 'modern thought'. The phrase
covered both developments in science, especially geology and
biology, and the growing challenge posed by a critical reading
of the Bible. Edmund Gosse has given us a vivid and moving
account of his Evangelical father's struggle to relate Darwinian
theory to his belief in the inspiration of the Bible and the
scientific accuracy of the book of Genesis. Gosse senior was a
scientist of some repute and was close enough to Charles
Darwin to be appraised by him of the theory of natural selection two years in advance of the publication of *Origin Of
Species*. His son tells us that 'every instinct in his intelligence
went out at first to greet the new light', but that the recollection
of the first chapter of Genesis led him to check this inclination
(Gosse:1986,103). After long reflection Philip Gosse devised a
theory of his own which he sincerely believed would point the
way to a satisfactory synthesis between the new knowledge
and belief in the literal accuracy of the biblical account of
creation. According to this theory, creation was a catastrophic
act which left the earth bearing the structural *appearance* of
great antiquity. Gosse was mortified to discover that no one
was willing to take the idea seriously. The press dismissed it
as suggesting that God hid the fossils in the rocks to tempt
geologists into infidelity, while his friend Charles Kingsley
wrote that he was unwilling 'to give up the painful and slow
conclusion of five and twenty years' study of geology, and
believe that God has written on the rocks one enormous and
superfluous lie' (Ibid:105). According to his son, Philip Gosse
interpreted his failure and public humiliation as a divine
chastisement and, from this time, became introverted and
alienated from a culture in which the new science played an
increasingly central role. Indeed, after his death the *British
Weekly* reported that Gosse had constantly studied prophecy
and 'read the *Times* daily, in order to see the decadence of the
nations, both Eastern and Western, in their downward
progress'.

Philip Gosse's rejection of evolution on the basis of a literalistic reading of the Genesis account of creation became a common position among conservative Evangelicals and was later to become one of the hallmarks of American Fundamentalism. However, notwithstanding the mythology which has come down to us concerning the conflict between religion and science at this time, Gosse's reaction was far from being the only option available to Evangelicals and, among intellectuals at least, it was not a common one. Evangelicals in science had already come to terms with geology and, refusing to allow scientific investigation to be fettered by a culture-bound reading of the Bible, they argued that the new knowledge obtained by means of the empirical study of phenomena should compel theologians to reconsider traditional interpretations of the book of Genesis. In fact, Evangelical scientists were among Darwin's foremost advocates in the second half of the nineteenth century. In the United States, the devout Christian botanist Asa Gray, who had devoted his life to science as a direct consequence of his understanding of Calvin's doctrine of the Christian calling, was the leading defender of evolution and ensured that the theory would get a fair hearing in the New World. Even Bishop Wilberforce, so often misrepresented as an obscurantist bigot, lamented the damage done to religion by the 'fussy energy with which men, narrow and feeble alike in faith and science, have bustled forth to reconcile all new discoveries in physics with the word of inspiration'. The Bishop was unequivocal in denouncing attempts to 'test the truth of natural science by the word of revelation'.

Of course evolutionary theory did raise profound theological and philosophical questions which were to engage the minds of Christian thinkers for the rest of the century. Darwin himself seems to have been well aware of the tremendous mythical power inherent within his theory and of the danger that the metaphor of natural selection might easily be absolutized as a depiction of reality itself. It is difficult, Darwin admitted, to avoid personifying nature, but 'I mean by Nature, only the aggregate action and product of many natural laws' (Livingstone:1987,47). This was exactly the point identified by Evangelical thinkers as representing the real challenge posed

by the theory of evolution. They were not concerned, like
Philip Gosse, to defend the idea of a young earth in the interests
of biblical literalism, since most of them had long since accepted that geological evidence pointed unerringly to an immensely enlarged time-span for the earth's history. What *did*
concern them was the reconstruction of natural theology in
such a way as to make possible an evolutionary teleology; this
was a strategy far more common than outright rejection of
Darwinian theory.

In time Darwin's 'mere metaphor' was lost from view and,
with the development of *social* Darwinism, evolution became
identified with a thoroughly naturalistic *Weltanschauung*.
When this occurred then the theory of evolution came to be
seen as symbolic of a profound cultural shift. The disturbing
effects of this change were felt by all religious people; traditional foundations for faith seemed shaken, old certainties
crumbled and left many believers 'stumbling up the altar stairs
in darkness' (Chadwick:1966,567).

How did Evangelicals react in this crisis of faith? Many
responded by falling back on an apologetic based almost
entirely upon a rigidly rational line of argument. A defence of
the faith which was believed to have routed the Deists a
century earlier was dusted down and pressed into service
against the new enemy. Charles Kingsley criticized Evangelicals' use of an outdated apologetic when, in *Alton Locke*, he
introduced a prison chaplain who attempts to win the artisan
hero of the book back to orthodox Christianity by lending him
'Paley's Evidences' and 'some tracts of the last generation
against Deism'. The Chartist Locke, who has read Strauss's *Das
Leben Jesu* and works by Emerson, reads the tracts and
comments that, like hundreds of others, he remained exactly
where he was before. The great mistake of the Evangelicals,
Kingsley implies, was that their rusty guns remained trained
on Voltaire and Paine at a time when quite different challenges
to faith needed to be faced and answered (Kingsley:1983,288).

Convinced that the acceptance of the data of revelation must
be total and uncritical, Evangelicals constructed an either/or
argument in which faith became almost inseparable from an
inerrant Bible. Thus Daniel Wilson wrote in 1861, 'You either

receive the Bible as the infallible Word of God, or you sink at once into infidelity.' Dean Burgon, in a series of sermons preached in Oxford in reply to *Essays And Reviews*, made the same point: 'Once admit the principle of fallibility into the inspired Word, and the whole becomes a bruised and rotten reed.' Burgon drew an analogy with one's feelings on discovering that a trusted friend was a liar and, unaware of the catastrophic consequences of such an apologetic, he said that 'after one proven falsehood, he would feel unable ever to trust that friend implicitly again' (Cameron:1982,18). This was a domino theory of apologetics: if just one statement in the Bible were shown to be false (on the basis of nineteenth-century definitions of truth and error), then the entire structure of revealed religion was doomed. This kind of apologetic was widely used in the 1860s and received definitive expression in H.P. Liddon's famous Bampton Lectures of 1866. Liddon argued that since Christ believed Moses to be the author of the Pentateuch and Jonah to have been swallowed by a fish, then modern denials of these facts imperilled not just the authority of the Bible, but that of Jesus himself. Such a position satisfied those already convinced that their faith was unassailable but for increasing numbers of people who were deeply troubled about the relationship between faith and modern thought, the results of such an apologetic were disastrous. When honest, thoughtful men and women were told that they must accept all or nothing, that capitulation to modern thought on a single point would involve the abandoning of Christianity altogether, then the intellectual travail involved in attempting to relate faith to a changing culture became a life-and-death struggle.

George Eliot, in a penetrating critique of this kind of apologetics, described it as suicidal. Reviewing the theology of Dr John Cumming, a well-known London preacher and the author of a string of apologetic works, the novelist commented that he appeared unable to conceive that doubt, instead of being damnable, might sometimes be 'the stamp of a truth-loving mind'. In words that cast a revealing light on her own struggles, she wrote that Cumming's Evangelicalism did not enable him even to conceive the condition of a mind 'perplext

in faith but pure in deeds', craving light, 'yearning for a faith
that will harmonize and cherish its highest powers and aspirations, but unable to find that faith in dogmatic Christianity'
(Eliot:1859:448).

There are many examples of prominent Victorian intellectuals who, faced with the radical choice presented to them by
Evangelical apologists, opted for agnosticism and, often at the
price of immense personal and family suffering, turned away
from the faith of their fathers. Leslie Stephen's belief that he
must accept every word in the Bible as literal truth or cease to
be a Christian led him to renounce his father's religion
(Chadwick:1970,113). Arnold Bennett explained a similar loss
of faith in a way that illustrates the impossible dilemma such
people faced when confronted by the apologist's either/or
choice:

> The empire of Christianity is crumbling because it has been attacked
> at . . . its sole weak point; the once universally accepted convention
> that the theory of the direct, divine inspiration of the Bible must not
> be questioned . . . From the moment when geologists demonstrate that
> the earth could not have been made in six days or six years or
> six-thousand years . . . from that moment the convention was doomed
> (Cox:1982,236).

Perhaps the most moving account of the failure of Evangelicalism to retain the allegiance of the rising generation of
Victorian intellectuals is found in Edmund Gosse's *Father And
Son*. Gosse relates how, having at last confessed to his father
the doubts he felt concerning the rigid system of belief in
which he had been reared, he was presented with an 'Everything or Nothing' choice in the form of a terrible letter in
which his father lamented the 'horrid, insidious infidelity'
which had taught him to evade the authority of Scripture
(Gosse:1986,250). The parting of the ways was inevitable and,
since no modification of the system was possible, the young
man abandoned Evangelicalism *in toto*. While Edmund
Gosse's objections to his father's religion centred on the doctrine of biblical inerrancy, they included the charge that
Evangelicalism suppressed aspects of human life and enjoy-
ment which are vital to a meaningful and satisfying existence
in this world:

It encourages a stern and ignorant spirit of condemnation; it throws altogether out of gear the healthy environment of the conscience; it invents virtues that are sterile and cruel; it invents sins which are no sins at all, but which darken the heaven of innocent joy with futile clouds of remorse. There is something horrible . . . in the fanaticism that can do nothing with this pathetic and futile existence of ours but treat it as if it were but the uncomfortable ante-chamber to a palace which no one has explored and of the plan of which we know absolutely nothing (Ibid:248).

It must be stressed that Gosse's account of his upbringing within the narrow confines of Plymouth Brethrenism should *not* be regarded as representative of Evangelicalism as a whole. And yet, his impassioned protest against his parents' devaluation of the aesthetic side of life, their exclusion of the imaginary and poetic from his upbringing, is not without relevance and challenge to the wider movement. Certainly by 1870 agnostics rather than Christians 'had the sense of being official, an intellectual establishment more powerful than the church establishment' (Cockshutt:1959,11).

A voice crying in the wilderness

The Evangelical reaction to 'modern thought' can be further illustrated by considering the extraordinary ministry of the Baptist preacher, Charles Haddon Spurgeon. He arrived in London five years before the publication of Darwin's *Origin of Species*, a representative not only of the staunchest Evangelicalism but of an older Calvinistic and Puritan tradition. Within weeks of beginning his ministry in 1854, the New Park Street Chapel, which had seemed in terminal decline prior to the arrival of the young pastor, was overflowing with people. Plans were laid to enlarge the building and while this was being done Spurgeon hired the Exeter Hall. By the time the chapel enlargement was completed it was found totally inadequate to accommodate the crowds flocking to hear the young preacher. Spurgeon went into the fields at Hackney and preached to a crowd of 10,000; then, when even the Exeter Hall proved unable to hold his regular Sunday congregation, he shocked both his Anglican friends and respectable Nonconformity by hiring the

Royal Surrey Gardens Music Hall on the South Bank of the
Thames. Sunday services in the Exeter Hall were one thing (at
least it had the hallowed association of the May Meetings), but
to preach in a Music Hall with its obvious links with worldly
entertainment was deeply shocking to many people. Yet when
Spurgeon arrived for the first service on Sunday, 19 October
1856, the 10,000-seat Hall was already crammed to capacity and
as many people again milled around outside seeking admission. The meeting ended in tragedy however, when, following
a false (and, Spurgeon believed, malicious) fire alarm, seven
people died in the stampede for the exits. Yet the disaster
seemed to rally public sympathy and support to the young
pastor; he continued to minister in the Music Hall for three years
before moving to the newly built Metropolitan Tabernacle in
South London which he packed with hearers for the next thirty
years. Chadwick rightly describes this as 'a preaching career
without parallel in modern history' (Chadwick:1966,418).

Spurgeon's sermons were published weekly for over half a
century; by 1865 they had obtained a circulation of 25,000 and
it has been estimated that by 1902 up to 300 million copies,
translated into at least 34 languages, had been sold. The sermons of C.H. Spurgeon literally circled the globe: Robert Louis
Stevenson described his Sundays in the South Sea Islands as
never complete without the 'inevitable' Spurgeon sermon,
while the preacher was deeply moved to learn that one of his
expositions was found with David Livingstone after his death,
annotated in the great man's own hand – 'Very good. D.L.'
Spurgeon's sermons were read by Vincent van Gogh and by
the theologian James Denney, who abandoned liberal theological views after reading them at the insistence of his young
wife.

How can we account for this phenomenal ministry which
began at the very point at which the doubts and anxieties
resulting from the emergence of the new sciences were being
experienced so acutely by thoughtful people? The reasons for
Spurgeon's success are many. He was a man of quite excep-
tional gifts. Testimonies to the sheer power of his oratory are
legion. When Augustine Birrell went to hear him he was

offered a seat in the topmost gallery between a woman eating an orange and a man sucking peppermints! As he was about to leave he was arrested by the voice of Spurgeon announcing the first hymn and, he wrote, 'I forgot all else.' Spurgeon's style and language may have offended George Eliot and Matthew Arnold but his supreme concern was to reach beyond the chapel respectability and to gain the ears of working people. Chadwick rightly describes Spurgeon as a preacher to the wastes of London, 'more brash, aggressive, public, biting, and worldly, because haunted by multitudes of souls athirst' (Chadwick:1966,421). Spurgeon took Edward Miall's laments concerning the influence of the 'aristocratic sentiment' on English religion very seriously and agreed with him that, from the point of view of effective mission, it was absurd that all forms of communication 'not approved by those who call themselves the respectable section of society' should be dismissed as 'unbecoming' or even as 'a desecration of revealed truth' (Miall:1849,199). Against the prevailing social trends of his time, Spurgeon deliberately distanced himself from the symbols of élite culture in an attempt to communicate to ordinary people. The editor of the *British Weekly* had no doubt that this was a factor in Spurgeon's success: 'We suspect,' he wrote, 'few educated people understand the almost incredible pleasure the masses have in hearing a loud, clear, pleasant voice break upon their ears.'

However, Spurgeon responded to Miall's analysis at another level: he not only spoke the language of common people, but identified publicly with many of their political aspirations. The extent of this commitment to radical politics is nowhere more evident than in a pamphlet he wrote and signed for distribution in South London during the election campaign of 1880:

> Are we to have another six years of Tory rule? . . . Are we to go on slaughtering and invading in order to obtain a scientific frontier and feeble neighbours? How many wars may we reckon on between now and 1886? . . . Let those who rejoice in war vote for the Tories . . . Shall all great questions of reform and progress be utterly neglected for years to come? They will be, unless true Liberals come to the front. In the name of Peace, Justice, Reform and Progress, muster your forces (Meredith:1973,65–6).

This passage illustrates Spurgeon's chronic opposition to Toryism and his distaste for the imperialistic spirit which he believed was bound up with it. He remained an implacable enemy of British imperialism and jingoism all his life and resisted the growing trend toward a civil religion given respectability by its association with Christian symbolism. In 1857, speaking to over 20,000 people at the Crystal Palace on the day of national mourning following the Indian Mutiny, he had the audacity to question Britain's role in India. In the same year, preaching at the annual meetings of the Baptist Missionary Society, he launched a withering attack on those who would glorify war and encourage the veneration of military heroes. The Gospel, he said, is a message of peace and when it has the success promised to it in Scripture, then 'wars *must* cease to the ends of the earth'. Spurgeon describes the appearance of the statues of military men in London as 'the trickery of an ignorant age, the gewgaws of a people who loved bloodshed despite their profession of religion'. He looks forward to the day when Nelson will be pulled down from his column and replaced with a statue of George Whitefield and the iron and brass of every statue standing in the city will be sold 'and the price thereof, cast at the apostles' feet, that they may make distribution as every man hath need'. Nearly a quarter of a century later his opposition to war is undiminished: we are 'still eager to test our ability to kill our fellowmen', he says in 1870, and, while mythical 'British Interests' are set up as the excuse for foreign adventures, 'the truth is that the national bulldog wants to fix his teeth into somebody's leg' (Meredith: 1973,96).

The editor of the *British Weekly* had no doubt that 'Spurgeon's theology was a main element in his lasting attraction'. In an obituary notice in 1892 he noted that Spurgeon was not alone in preaching the old, dogmatic Calvinism with success among the masses: James Wells, whose Calvinism was stricter than that of the pastor of the Metropolitan Tabernacle, had amazing responsiveness to his message in the 'damp, low-lying, thickly-peopled, struggling regions' of the Metropolis and 'had such a funeral as South London had never seen before'. How was it that these men, preaching the sovereignty of divine grace in the form of Calvin's now despised doctrine of election, attracted the poor and deprived who so signally ignored what was on offer in more fashionable congregations? 'Mr Spurgeon's hearers,' said the editorial, 'had many of them missed all the prizes of life; but God did not choose them for the reasons that move men's preference, else their case were hopeless.' He went on:

> Many a poor girl with the love of CHRIST and goodness in her heart, working her fingers to the bone for a pittance that just keeps her alive, with the temptation of the streets around her, and the river beside her, listened with all her soul when she heard that CHRIST'S sheep could never perish.

However, as Spurgeon's celebrity increased so did the middle-class make up of his audience. One witness present at a Sunday evening service in 1878 at which the regular congregation had been asked to stay away in order to encourage outsiders to come, noted, 'We do not observe any of the very poor . . . We find no one as low as a working man, no one who follows any liberal or learned profession' (Fullerton:1934,150–1). By the 1880s a visit to the Tabernacle had become part of the tourist itinerary, as is evidenced by the Scotsman who said he 'dinna want to die until he gang to London to see Madame Tussaud's and hear Mr Spurgeon'. What attracted *these* people to a preacher who spoke with such dogmatic assurance? A study of the sermons Spurgeon preached during the last ten years of his life reveals a constant preoccupation with 'modern thought'. Spurgeon's ministry exactly mirrors the cultural changes which, as we have seen, became increasingly evident from mid-century onwards. Whereas his early London ministry identified Romanism and Puseyism as the main enemies of the Gospel, by 1880 the traditional threat to the Protestant religion has been overshadowed by a new challenge which endangers not merely Protestantism, but the foundations of all religious belief. He laments the tendency of modern thought to evade the 'simple matters of fact upon which our religion is built'. Whereas three of four 'plain facts' constitute the Gospel, modern people seem to be forever craving 'some fresh fantasia'; they would 'tear out the bowels of truth, and give us a carcass stuffed with hypotheses, speculations, and larger hopes'. Spurgeon's concept of science is essentially Baconian and he shared the general alarm at the way in which modern theology was abandoning the eighteenth-century apologetic: 'In this age all the ships in the waters are pulling up their anchors; they are drifting with the tide; they are driven by every wind.' His sermons throughout the 1880s leave the impression that he and his opponents inhabited quite different thought-worlds; while they were baffled by his success, he sees modern thought, with its characteristic critical questioning, as 'a sheer, clear waste of time'. For Spurgeon evolution has become the symbol of all that is wrong with the modern world and occasionally he descends to the level of lampooning the theory in a manner that foreshadows the kind of treatment it was later to receive at the hands of the Fundamentalists: 'The god of modern thought is a monkey. If those who believed in evolution said their prayers rightly, they would begin them with "Our Father, which art up a tree".'

In fairness it must be said that, by the 1880s, Spurgeon was not contending with a scientific theory, but with full-blown Social-Darwinism with all its hubristic ramifications for Victorian ethics and economics. Indeed, the very imperialism which he so vigorously opposed was itself a fruit of the doctrine of the survival of the fittest, and his detestation of evolution must be seen in this light. Nonetheless, such language contributed to the widening of the gap by which popular Evangelicalism was divided from those who were now shaping modern culture and it made much more difficult the task of other representatives of the Evangelical tradition who sought to relate historic Christianity to the findings of genuine science.

Spurgeon's ministry provided believers with protection from the alarming winds which seemed to be blowing from all directions in Victorian Britain. The stiffest opposition to biblical criticism came from the great Victorian preachers, Spurgeon, Joseph Parker and Alexander MacLaren. Parker said in 1893: 'I am jealous lest the Bible should in any sense be made a priest's book . . . Have we to await a communication from Tübingen or a telegram from Oxford, before we can read the Bible?' (Glover:1954:256f). Spurgeon, ever a man of the people, expressed similar opposition to the new 'priesthood of scholarship'. When someone urged him to preach in a style that would alienate the 'mob' at Newington and replace them with the élite, Spurgeon dismissed him as a 'miserable snob'. His resistance to modern thought was in considerable measure *pastorally* motivated: if the authority of the Bible were destroyed what would the preacher have had to offer the thousands of ordinary people who crammed the Tabernacle every Sunday for thirty years? The attraction of his ministry was that, in an age of unprecedented doubt, it offered stability, certainty, continuity. Here was a man who could say with utter sincerity, as Spurgeon did in the last year of his life, '. . . the Gospel we preached forty years ago we will still preach in forty years time if we are still alive.'

However, while Spurgeon belonged to the tradition of world-transformative Christianity which looked with confidence to a time when the Gospel would renew the nations, in the closing decade of his life his sermons reveal an unmistakable increase in pessimism. In the Baptist Missionary Society sermon of 1858 he had been able to anticipate the cessation of wars as the Gospel of peace becomes the controlling influence in the affairs of the nations, but in the closing years of his life a far more negative eschatology comes to the fore and he criticizes those 'sanguine brethren' who maintain the very hope he had once preached. Spurgeon says that he now looks for the darkening down of things; the state of mankind, however improved politically, may yet grow worse and worse spiritually. At the time of his death the *British Weekly* reported, with evident surprise, that, not long before the end, the pastor of the Metropolitan Tabernacle had placed his signature on a 'manifesto' which concluded with the words, 'Our hope is in the Personal, Pre-millennial, return of the Lord Jesus Christ in Glory.'

New directions in evangelism

A sense of gloom became widespread in the 1880s. J.C. Ryle, who had become the first Bishop of Liverpool in 1880, spoke during a triennial visit in his Cathedral ten years later of the seemingly hopeless condition of the Church of England; the times were dangerous, he said, 'the air filled with vain agnosticism and unbelief, faith languishing and dwindling everywhere, and looking ready to die'. Ryle and Spurgeon were both Calvinists who looked back on the eighteenth-century Revival as the golden age of Evangelicalism and they shared a sense of despair at the intellectual trends which appeared so threatening by the last quarter of the century. It was clear that the traditional Christian worldview no longer provided a generally accepted framework for contemporary culture, that it was being replaced by a *Weltanschauung* derived from sources which appeared hostile to all religious belief.

Anglican Evangelicals made considerable efforts to reach the poor in the inner cities by means of services held in secular buildings. An interesting testimony to the ineffectiveness of such methods is provided by Charles Dickens who recorded his impressions of two visits to the Britannia Theatre in Hoxton. On Saturday night he joined the regular audience to watch a pantomime and reckoned that two thousand people were present, mostly mechanics, dockers, petty tradesmen, and the like. They were neither clean nor 'choice' in their lives or conversation, he says. The following night the theatre had been hired by Evangelicals and Dickens returned in order to 'compare the play on Saturday evening with the preaching on Sunday evening'. The second-night crowd was considerably larger than that of Saturday but, Dickens says, the audiences on the two evenings consisted of entirely different sorts of people. The great mass of the usual patrons of the Britannia Theatre had 'decidedly and unquestionably stayed away' on Sunday night. The new crowd was an imported one, made up of 'respectable strangers attracted by curiosity, and drafts from the regular congregations of various chapels'. The contrast was so marked that Dickens expressed impatience with the preacher's address to an imaginary outcast, since the whole appearance of this Sunday crowd made obvious their 'respectable character' (Dickens:n.d.,39–43).

Hugh McLeod has described the growth of a working-class ethos and culture in London marked by 'the concentration of knowledge, responsibility and personal ties within a small area, and lack of interest in events outside'. This working-class parochialism was imposed by the exigencies of the struggle to keep body and soul together; it was a physical and psychical self-defence, 'the demarkation of a limited area within which those at the lower end of a highly stratified society could ensure for themselves a degree of status and recognition' (McLeod:1974,44). Given the growth of this working-class culture, self-improvers, bookworms, or those who showed sympathy toward middle-class religious organizations, were liable to be ostracized. According to McLeod, the striking thing about urbanization was not that its effect on religious practice was uniform, but that it created a series of separate worlds marked by radically different styles of life. He concludes:

> When the members of a community are divided into classes, always separate and often antagonistic, meeting only in relations of authority and subordination, it is futile to expect that they will meet in the same church. The great majority of the London working class were not, therefore, potential converts to the Church of England or to the denominations ... dominated by the middle class, though outstanding ministers in those denominations could still win some working-class following (Ibid:281).

Neither theatre-based services nor successive waves of American-inspired revivalism in the 1870s were able to overcome the resistance of those outside the churches. Revivalist techniques developed in the context of camp meetings on the American frontier had been introduced into Britain earlier in the century by men like Calvin Colton and Charles Finney. The theology which underlay revivalism of this type involved a distinctively modern view of man's relation to the supernatural; revival ceased to be a *divine* act and became something within the control of human beings. Revivals could be produced, or promoted, by human agency. The emergence of this idea, which would have been inconceivable to the eighteenth-century evangelists, may be another indicator that 'the classical Protestant theology of the spiritual life was losing its hold on Western culture' (Kent:1978,21). This view is confirmed by the rapidity with which the revivalism of the American evangelist D.L. Moody supplanted the older Evangelical understanding of

revivals following his arrival in Britain in 1873. Moody's evangelistic techniques were accepted by British Evangelicals not
only in the great urban centres, but in rural Scotland. Thus, we
find an evangelist conducting meetings in Kintyre in 1897 'on
bright attractive lines with plenty of singing' from Sankey's
Hymn Book, short prayers, a brief message, and the characteristic 'after meeting' when 'the anxious were invited to enter
the enquiry room' (Carson:1966,21). Even in the land of John
Knox the solution to the problem of the 'lapsed masses' (which
was, Carson tells us, much discussed in Campbelltown prior to
these meetings), was now seen to rest in the use of humanly-
devised techniques and the preaching of a message shorn of the
doctrinal content of the older, Reformed traditions. In welcoming Moody's revivalism, British Evangelicals were involved in
a desperate attempt to retain their hold on a culture which was
increasingly adrift from Christian moorings. Thus, Balleine
explains the remarkable *volte face* which enabled Anglicans,
who had earlier refused to 'fraternize with Anabaptists', to
welcome with open arms a Chicago businessman whose knowledge of theology was minimal and whose evangelism involved
startling innovations, as follows: '. . . the visit of this breezy
layman from America helped Churchmen and Nonconformists
to see how much they had in common, and how much unity was
needed among the Christian forces in a land where irreligion
was winning so many victories' (Balleine:1908,254).

The Moody mission in Glasgow in 1873 left the working
classes untouched while offering the middle-class Evangelical
constituency the reassurance it sought at a time when its
worldview was under serious threat from modern thought.
The failure of revivalism to reach the working class was also
evident in the London meetings of 1875. Although the mission
was based in Islington, the poorer inhabitants of the district
simply would not come. At the same time, the location was a
deterrent to the upper classes, with the result that, as Lord
Shaftesbury realized, the meetings were turning into a display
of middle-class pietism. The *Spectator* made the same point:
Moody was simply preaching to the converted, most of whom
'have quite as good if not better teaching than Moody and
Sankey can give'. People beset by intellectual doubts were

even less likely to go to the Great Hall in Islington when the *Spectator* reported that the evangelists, although sincere and good men, had no knowledge of 'the difficulties which beset the faith of modern Christians' but seemed to believe that 'the right way to get over any difficulties . . . is to get up some how or other a sufficient tide of emotion to float ordinary persons over them' (Kent:1978,149).

The year 1875 not only saw the climax of Moody's work in Britain, but the convening of a conference in Brighton for the 'deepening of spiritual life' under the leadership of another American, Robert Pearsall Smith. Together with his wife, Hannah Whitall Smith, he stressed a 'second blessing' experience by means of which the Christian might attain to victory over the power of sin, inward rest of soul, and a blissful feeling of happiness. The new emphasis was summed up in the title of Mrs Smith's best-selling book, *The Christian's Secret Of A Happy Life*. The social character of this movement is revealed by a report that the 'besetting sins' most frequently confessed during the Smiths' ministry in England were 'a tattling tongue, angry looks, viciousness on the croquet lawn, impatience with servants' (Frank:1986,142).

Despite vigorous protests from a few Evangelical leaders, hundreds of prominent Christians drank in the new doctrines. J.C. Ryle wrote a staunch defence of the traditional understanding of sanctification in which he observed that thousands crowded to hear novel teachings and displayed an unhealthy appetite for 'a sort of spasmodic and hysterical Christianity'. The religious life of many of his fellow-Evangelicals seemed to the Bishop of Liverpool to consist of 'spiritual dram-drinking' and he deplored the tendency to focus on the personal and subjective aspects of Christianity to the exclusion of its social and objective character. Biblical holiness, Ryle insisted, did *not* lead to the neglect of social duties; it was *not* 'a mere hot-house plant which can thrive only under shelter, but a strong, hardy thing which can flourish in every relation of life' (Ryle:1952,26). Yet the tide was flowing against Ryle and his traditional, Puritan view of holiness, and he recognized that his protests were unlikely to arrest the movement toward the privatization and marginalization of Evangelical religion which he saw as the end-products of the new approach to Christian holiness.

The General next to God

Clearly we have reached a point in the story at which the tradition of world-transformative Christianity suffered partial eclipse within Evangelicalism. The earlier vision expressed in classic form in Isaac Watts' hymn, 'Jesus shall reign where'er the sun/Doth his successive journeys run', faded from the memories of a generation taught to sing a very different type of song by Ira Sankey. As they retreated before the seemingly irresistible advance of modern thought, many Evangelicals sang, 'Hold the fort, for I am coming', their vision of what the Gospel might achieve now limited to the defence of an outpost stranded in enemy territory, to be held until the Second Advent of Christ.

However, this is by no means the whole story. Powerful voices were raised in protest at such timidity and social conformism. For example, Andrew Mearns drew attention to conditions in the slums in his *The Bitter Cry of Outcast London*. The public outcry this provoked led directly to a Royal Commission on the Housing of the Poor which laid the foundation for modern social legislation. His information was supplied by the agents of the London City Mission and Baptists like Archibald Brown of the East London Tabernacle, and it led him to conclude that preaching was foredoomed if it ignored the fact that social conditions could determine people's response to the Gospel. A message of individual salvation made little sense while a nation which prided itself as being 'Christian' condemned people to live like the 'uncleanest of brute beasts'. To the thousands who were hopelessly trapped in fever dens, the gospel of 'self help' was a cruel mockery, while an Evangelicalism which refused to address the 'social question' was little better. Mearns argued that unless and until the state intervened to bring an end to the iniquitous traffic in human lives which resulted from the doctrine of *laissez faire*, Christian evangelists had no chance of success in the slums.

The impact of the *Bitter Cry* was immense. Respectable Britain, still clinging to the illusion of being a Christian nation with a God-given destiny to enlighten and civilize the heathen at the antipodes, was appalled by the revelation that to ask whether couples in the slums were married only brought a smile at the questioner's simplicity. Even worse, Mearns reported that incest was common and that 'no form of vice and sensuality causes surprise or attracts attention' (Mearns: 1883,61). This was an affront to Victorian cultural pride; behaviour which might be excused in 'savages' who belonged lower in the scale of evolutionary development than western people, was found to be common at the heart of Victoria's Empire!

Mearns' *Bitter Cry* played a significant part in moulding the social vision of William Booth, the founder of the Salvation Army. Since his conversion in 1844 Booth had dedicated his life to the evangelization of the poor. Inspired by the example of John Wesley, he took seriously the famous instruction to go 'to those who need you most'. By one of those peculiar ironies which are always occurring in religious history, the churches descended from Wesley were unable to contain this man. Booth's evangelistic passion brought him into conflict with the chapel respectability in Nottingham when, driving a shabby procession of outcasts into the evening service, he faced the ire of the astounded mill managers and shopkeepers who protested this invasion of their pews. Years later Booth's wife, Catherine, replied to a gentleman who insisted that there was much love for Christ to be found in middle-class churches, 'Yes, for their idealistic Saviour. But suppose Jesus was to come to your chapel as He went about Palestine, with a carpenter's coat on, or ... all over perspiration and dust with travel, where would your chapel steward put him to sit?' (Magnusson: 1977,170). She was later to describe fashionable religion as 'despicable'.

The conditions the Salvationists discovered in outcast London compelled a re-evaluation of their philosophy and practice of evangelism. People motivated by the compassion of Christ to the extent that the Booths were simply could not remain indifferent to the physical sufferings of the poor. It also became clear to them that, despite daring innovations in evangelistic technique, there were segments of the population in the slums which seemed impervious to all their soul-winning efforts. Booth became increasingly aware that sin could not be dealt with adequately as long as the social factors which gave rise to it were ignored; a message of salvation must address the problems raised by the *Bitter Cry*.

W.T. Stead, editor of the *Pall Mall Gazette*, provided a direct link between Andrew Mearns' work and William Booth's *In Darkest England And The Way Out* (1890). In an editorial, Stead had drawn attention to Mearns' findings and challenged his readers to face the need for far-reaching reforms in order to remedy the social injustices suffered by the poor. He suggested that 'the grim Florentine' might have added to his visions of the horrors of hell 'by a sojourn in a London slum' (Wohl,ed.:1970,82). In language which his friend Catherine Booth would certainly have approved, Stead went on to ask, 'Why all this apparatus of temples and meeting houses to save men from perdition in the world which is to come, while never a helping hand is stretched out to save them from the inferno of their present life?' (Ibid:83). When Booth's *In Darkest England* appeared, Stead's influence was obvious: within a few pages there is a reference to 'Dante's Hell' with the comment that anyone walking through 'the shambles of our civilization needs no such fantastic images of the poet to teach him horror'. Booth acknowledges a link between the living hell of the slums and the spread of atheism and says that, when surveying the utter despair and hopelessness of the poor, it often seemed *to him* 'as if God were no longer in his world' (Booth:1890,13).

Given this admission, it is not surprising that Booth, like Mearns, Guthrie and Miall before him, endeavoured to develop a social ethic consistent with his Evangelicalism. His commitment to evangelism never wavered and he continued to affirm the salvation of men's souls as his highest goal, yet he repeatedly argues that, given the dreadful conditions of outcast London, action to change people's environment must take priority over the preaching of a message of individual salvation. When successive generations had grown up amid the horrors of the slums, there developed a *heredity* of incapacity which created thousands of people 'disinherited before their birth of their share of the average intelligence of mankind' (Ibid:44). Booth cites an example:

> The bastard of a harlot, born in a brothel, suckled on gin, and familiar from earliest infancy with all the bestialities of debauch, violated before she is twelve, and driven out into the streets by her mother a year or two later, what chance is there for such a girl in this world – I say nothing about the next? (Ibid:47).

Booth recognized that while a favourable environment might not change a person's heart or transform his nature (Catherine Booth would doubtless have pointed to middle-class religiosity as evidence of that!), the desperate conditions of the slums might 'render it absolutely impossible' for a person to escape (Ibid:86). Consequently the scheme of social reform proposed in *Darkest England* raised issues of an overtly political nature. Like the *Bitter Cry* it called into question *laissez faire* economic theory. Booth is quite explicit about this: whereas, he says, his scheme may easily be harmonized with socialism, it is in irreconcilable conflict with 'those anti-Christian economists who hold that it is an offence against the doctrine of the survival of the fittest to try to save the weakest from going to the wall, and who believe that when a man is down it is the supreme duty of a self-regarding society to jump upon him' (Ibid:18). The book contains devastating criticisms of the social structure of Victorian Britain and of Evangelical connivance in a system which creates a 'waste continent of humanity', three million enslaved people from Plymouth to Peterhead (Ibid:20). In attacking the iniquity of the poor-law system, which provided the unemployed with a night's shelter in exchange for stone-breaking, Booth, like Miall, condemns a one-sided Evangelical charity: half a ton of stone, he says, in exchange for partially relieving the pangs of hunger is 'an outrage which, if we read of its occurring in Russia or Siberia would find Exeter Hall crowded with an indignant audience' (Ibid:70).

While explicit in his opposition to unbridled capitalism, Booth was less sure about his relation to emergent socialism. He can declare that he does not oppose those who seek the radical restructuring of society and he declares strong support for the principle of co-operation: 'I am a strong believer in

co-operation . . . I don't see how any specific re-adjustment of
the social and economic relations between classes . . . can be
effected except by the gradual substitution of cooperative
associations for the present wages system' (Ibid:78). Yet Booth
is essentially a pragmatist with little sympathy for utopian
visions. He will not oppose 'any short cut to the Millennium
that is compatible with the Ten Commandments' but, he says,
'at our shelters last night were a thousand hungry, workless
people. I want to know what to do with them?' (Ibid:79). The
following passage captures the essence of Booth's thought:

> The individualist tells me that the free play of Natural Laws governing
> the struggle for existence will result in the Survival of the Fittest, and
> that in the course of a few ages . . . a much nobler type will be evolved.
> But meanwhile what is to become of John Jones? The Socialist tells me
> that the great Social Revolution is looming large on the horizon. In the
> good time coming . . . all stomachs will be filled . . . It may be so, but
> in the meantime here is John Jones growing more impatient than ever
> because hungrier, who wonders if he is to wait for a dinner until the
> Social Revolution has arrived. What are we to do with John Jones?
> (Ibid:77–8).

Booth had as little patience with utopian dreamers of Right or
Left as he had with religious people who dispensed opium to
the poor in the form of the promise of heaven. Religious cant
'which rids itself of all the importunity of suffering humanity
by drawing unnegotiable bills payable on the other side of the
grave, is not more impracticable than the Socialistic clap-trap
which postpones all redress of human suffering until after the
general overturn'. Pietistic religion and visionary socialism are
bracketed together: both 'take refuge in the Future to escape a
solution to the problems of the Present' – and for John Jones it
really matters little whether that Future is on this side of the
grave or the other (Ibid:80). In effect, Booth *accepts* Marx's
critique of religion, but then turns it against a visionary socialism which places an almost religious faith in history and leaves
John Jones wondering where the next meal will come from.

Few Christians in the history of the church have demonstrated the compassion of Christ in lives of self-sacrificing
service more consistently than William and Catherine Booth.
In 1912, as the sightless General lay dying, his thoughts were
still filled with the plight of derelict humanity and he extracted

a promise from his son to do more for the homeless (Collier: 1968,221). Yet while Booth's concern for the suffering sprang from a heart which had experienced the reality of the love of Christ, it was not integrated theologically within the central objectives of the Christian mission and so remained in uneasy tension with the prime task of saving souls. This inability to unite the personal and social aspects of religion, to see mission as embracing both the declaration of the word of God and the practice of deeds which demonstrate the love and justice of God, remained one of Evangelicalism's consistent, and most damaging, failures.

The seriousness of this failure was recognized by the editor of the *British Weekly*, W. Robertson Nicoll. In a perceptive editorial on the subject of the church and the labour movement, published in the year that *Darkest England* appeared, he warned that to sneer at the emerging labour movement would be folly of the most mischievous kind. At a time when working men were becoming aware of their political strength, the attitude of the churches toward their demands would be likely to determine the extent to which Christianity would influence this sector of society in the future. Yet, if the past was anything to go by, the omens were not good: the church stood arraigned before the country, Nicoll says, for not declaring the whole counsel of Christ upon wealth. Under no honest interpretation of the words of Jesus can the Christian millionaire be justified and in any church governed by Christ's will 'the scorn reserved at present for the dissolute and the criminal would flash with even greater intensity on the covetous'. In words that were directly relevant to Evangelicalism's failure to confront the social question, he wrote,

> Christ, in his jealousy for the poor, insisted first of all that they should have justice. Justice, not generosity, is the specific virtue of the kingdom of God. Justice is far harder and more exacting than generosity. Generosity pledges one to nothing, and has for its reward an inward glow of self-approval. But every act of justice implies a deliberate judgement on our own claims as well as those of our neighbours. Whatever concession that judgement has forced upon us becomes henceforth a binding law of life that must govern every day, and which rewards us with no thrill of complacency for our obedience.

While Nicoll concludes that the church is bound 'to sympa-
thize with the aspirations of the people for a warmer and
kinder life', he refuses to identify social transformation as the
summum bonum of the Gospel. The churches must stand beside
the poor and identify unreservedly with their demands for
justice, but they must then ask 'how such a life can ever be
found and kept without CHRIST'. The transformation of society according to the demands of justice will not make the
central questions of the Gospel less important than before, but
will enhance their relevance and urgency. At the close of the
twentieth century we can perhaps appreciate Nicoll's claim: 'It
will be a poor triumph if toilers succeed in asserting the right
to eat, to sleep, to indulge passion, and to go down to graves
of lust.' Men, he says, have a nobler destiny. 'They will seek to
make the temporal life brighter, richer in opportunity than it
has been. But even in this they will succeed only as they realize
their place in that eternal and divine kingdom which will
remain when all earthly hours, whether of labour or of rest, are
run' (Nicoll:1890).

Evangelical apologetics in an age of doubt

While noting the weakness of Evangelical apologetics in relation to modern thought throughout the second half of the
nineteenth century, we have also seen that there were orthodox Christians who engaged in constructive dialogue with the
leaders of the new science. These devout Christian scholars
retained a clear commitment to the biblical faith, yet were
willing to listen to the thinkers and scientists who were now
shaping contemporary culture.

It is important to add that, by the end of the nineteenth
century Evangelicals were becoming painfully aware that their
hold over the middle class was slowly, but unmistakably,
beginning to weaken. In 1887 it was reported that statistics
from all parts of Britain showed that the Nonconformist denominations were 'either standing still or losing ground'.
Many children of devout Nonconformist families were either
turning away from the churches altogether, or were defecting

to Anglicanism. A correspondent to the *British Weekly* reported a trend in Scotland toward using Sundays for socializing; people passed through his town in their best clothes en route to friends with whom they spent the Lord's Day. Railway excursions, begun, ironically, in 1841 by the Baptist, Thomas Cook, and the attraction of cycle-rides into the countryside, weakened the hold of the chapels on the young. 'The bicycle,' said a worried minister, 'is doing more to abolish churchgoing, and so . . . to undermine Christianity, than any other social force' (Inglis:1963,75). Denominational leaders like R.W. Dale fretted about the long-term consequences of the changes they were witnessing. Dale had voiced his own criticisms of the eighteenth-century Revival which, he believed, had filled Congregational churches with converts who knew nothing of the traditions of Puritan Independency. Yet now the Evangelical tradition stemming from the Great Awakening was *itself* exhausted, as was clear from the worldliness which so evidently marked the lives of the rising generation within the churches.

One response to this situation was, as we have already seen, to opt for the privatization of faith and retreat to the apparent security of the ghetto. This may be designated as an anti-modernist reaction which, in its extreme forms, can be called the cult of 'Christ-against-western-culture'. However, an important group of theologians set about constructing an apologetic for orthodox Christianity which attempted to take very seriously the whole range of problems and questions raised by the advent of modern scientific and historical thought. In the United States this kind of response is exemplified by the Baptist theologian Augustus Strong. In the preface to his widely used *Systematic Theology*, Strong could affirm that neither evolution nor higher criticism held any terrors 'to one who regards them as parts of Christ's creating and educating process' (Strong:1907,vii). On his seventieth birthday Strong could write that the personal experience of union with Christ had enabled him to see 'in science and philosophy the teaching of my Lord'. Unlike the British apologists of the 1860s, he refused to stake the Christian faith on the correctness of the Bible in matters unrelated to the salvation of mankind: 'I open my mind to the evidence. I do not prejudge the case. I refuse

to impose upon students for the ministry the dogma of absolute inerrancy . . .' (Strong:1899,126–7). Thus, prior to the
Fundamentalist controversies in the 1920s a dialogical approach to modern thought was a valid and respected position
within American Evangelicalism.

In Britain the most distinguished representatives of this
critical dialogue with modernity were the Scottish theologians
James Orr and James Denney. They clearly recognized the
urgent need for a new apologetic which would respond hon-
estly and intelligently to the questions with which a scientific
culture confronted the Christian faith. Both men were fully
convinced, as Denney put it, that 'the attempt to appreciate the
mind of our time is forced upon us' since there are 'latent
presuppositions of the modern mind' which preclude its
understanding the conceptions of forgiveness and atonement
which lay at the heart of the Gospel (Denney:1903:18–19).
Denney recognized that the modern worldview simply left no
room for Christ and his work as Christian experience knows
them and it had become imperative that evangelism take
proper account of 'the mind that is around us'. The Christian
preacher *must* understand modernity if he is to have any
chance of liberating the minds of people who are liable to react
to traditional teaching with 'instinctive antipathy'. At the same
time, Denney refused to accept the presuppositions of modernity and baptize them as the new revelation of truth; the
understanding of the modern mind is a means to an end,
namely, the exposure of its inadequacies in the light of Christ
and the summons to conversion as modern people are made
aware of wider dimensions of reality than could be perceived
within a secular framework of understanding.

Like Strong, both men accepted the theory of evolution and
the historico-critical study of the Bible without anxiety. Orr
acknowledged that the 'much derided criticism' had brought
great benefits in that it enabled Christians to read the Bible in
a more natural way, with proper regard to the progressive
character of revelation (Orr:n.d.,317). Orr was a major contributor to the series of volumes which eventually gave their
name to the movement known as 'Fundamentalism'; yet even
in this context he insists that biblical criticism 'must have its

rights' and says that Christians should receive with thankfulness the light which science can throw on 'the composition or the authority or the age of these (biblical) books' (*Fundamentals*:n.d.,IX/33). Orr said that a doctrine of Scripture 'adapted to the needs of the hour in harmonising the demands at once of science and faith' was the most clamant want in theology (Orr:n.d.,352). Neither Orr nor Denney was prepared to affirm biblical inerrancy: attempts to demonstrate the reliability of biblical minutiae were suicidal, Orr said, while Denney saw the inspiration of Scripture solely in relation to its salvific purpose. The Bible did not offer, 'unless by accident, and then with no peculiar authority, a single fact of any description to any human science' (Denney:1891,354). Aware of the widespread feeling among intellectuals that religious belief had become irrational and impossible, Orr and Denney were anxious to insist on the Lordship of Christ over the whole of culture and they made a valiant effort to construct a new defence for Christian belief which would ensure that it could not be easily dismissed among those whom Schleiermacher had called the 'cultured despisers' of religion.

It should be added that for James Orr the most difficult task facing the church if it was to retain its legitimacy in the minds of men in the twentieth century, was that of bringing Christianity as 'an applied power on the life and conditions of society'. The church must

> set itself as it has never yet done to master the meaning of 'the mind of Christ' and to achieve the translation of that mind into the whole practical life of the age – into laws, institutions, commerce, literature, art; into domestic, civil, social, and political relations; into national and international doings – in this sense to bring in the kingdom of God among men (Orr:n.d.,353).

It was a noble vision and it reminds us of the eschatological hope of earlier Evangelicals a century before. Yet it did not long survive among Orr's contemporaries. His call to take a positive approach in bearing witness to Christ in the context of modern western culture was soon to be drowned out by gunfire and, amid the post-war traumas, Evangelicals forgot his words, lost sight of his world-transformative vision and neglected the task of apologetics which he and Denney had pioneered. Indeed, even as these Scottish theologians were urging the necessity of addressing modern people in intelligible terms, the Cambridge University Christian Union was relying upon an American revivalist whose evangelism was characterized by an emotional sentimentality. As a soloist sang a song with the words 'Tell Mother I'll Be There', Charles Alexander asked undergraduates to stand if they wished to meet their mothers in heaven (Pollock:1953,156–7). The Christian Union had clearly abandoned any attempt to speak the word of God meaningfully in a university permeated by secular thought and a mission which resorted to such frankly subjectivistic techniques was bound to confirm the intelligentsia in their belief that religious faith was irrational and impossible.

4

Decline and Resurgence:
Twentieth-Century Evangelicalism

By the close of the nineteenth century there were increasing references in the religious press to 'old' and 'new' Evangelicals. The former referred to those who opted for the defence and conservation of traditional formulations of belief while the latter was used to describe those who sought some accommodation with modernity. Participants in this debate still recognized each other as fellow-Evangelicals, but it contained the seeds of a coming schism in which antagonistic parties were to be identified by exclusive concern with *either* the social *or* the personal dimensions of religion.

However, with the outbreak of the First World War in August, 1914, the internal problems facing this tradition paled into insignificance in the light of a cultural crisis of truly global proportions. Taken-for-granted assumptions of all kinds were undermined and swept away by the terrible carnage in Europe. The World Missionary Conference in Edinburgh in 1910 operated on the basis of a clear distinction between the 'evangelized' parts of the world (Europe and America) and those that were 'unevangelized'. Yet the claim underlying this neat division, that the western world was a 'high' culture, shaped by the Christian message, appeared utterly incredible as the fields of France were drenched with European blood. At the same time, humanist-inspired visions of progress underwritten by faith in the evolutionary development of the species, were also shattered by the War. The Russian philosopher Nicholas Berdyaev was to comment that the conflict of 1914–18 was a ghastly 'revelation of evil' which uncovered 'the superficiality of the process of humanization' and showed how fragile was 'the layer of human society which had really been affected by humanizing forces' (Berdyaev:1935,15). No single group, certainly not Evangelical Christians, could lay claim to easy answers to the desperate questions raised by the War.

In their attitude to the conflict, Evangelicals differed little from other churchmen whose mood fluctuated between that of the Just War and the Crusade. No voice remotely similar to that of C.H. Spurgeon's was to be heard among Evangelicals between 1914 and 1918. G. Campbell Morgan, a leading Evangelical minister, preached what his biographer calls a 'war sermon' in London's Westminster Chapel on 30 August 1914. As he contemplated the twenty million men under arms, he uttered the following words: 'These lonely men are massed as ammunition on the one hand, as bulwarks on the other. If the Bible revelation is to be trusted, the sign of the Cross is on every man that marches to his death' (Harries:1930,127). This is clearly *crusading* language. Dr Morgan, who had earlier professed himself a pacifist and had refused to allow toy soldiers in his children's nursery, gave uncritical support to the Allied cause and turned his central London church into a 'marked centre of patriotic enthusiasm'. Another prominent Evangelical, E.J. Poole-Connor, who confessed absolute loyalty to the Spurgeonic tradition in doctrine, seemed unaware of his hero's abhorrence of war. Speaking of the Armaggedon across the Channel, he said that the members of his London church had 'entrusted their beloved sons, who have responded to their country's call, to God's care'. Meanwhile, those who remained at home gave 'particular emphasis to the Second Coming' (Fountain:1966,116–7). In their attitudes toward modern warfare (including the prospect of nuclear war), most twentieth-century Evangelicals were to take their cue from Campbell Morgan and Poole-Connor rather than from C.H. Spurgeon.

The dark age

The experience of the War served to widen the gap between 'old' and 'new' Evangelicals. Those of liberal inclination

returned from the trenches convinced that the need for Christians to address the socio-political questions facing the modern
world was more urgent than ever. By contrast, the conservatives (as they were to become known) now turned away from
the world and toward the one area where hope and optimism
could still flourish: the realm of the individual soul, the sphere
of *private* religion. George Marsden's comment concerning
American Evangelicals in the immediate post-war period ap-
plies equally to their British brothers: the light of optimism still
prevailed in the Evangelical outlook, only now 'it shone on the
individual rather than on the culture' (Marsden:1980,101).

The 1920s were to witness the emergence of Fundamentalism in the United States. This was essentially an *American*
phenomenon, resulting from a constellation of cultural factors
peculiar to the history of the United States. Consequently,
when the Fundamentalist battles raged in America very few
British Evangelicals were willing to 'rally to the battle cry'
(Ibid:222). While the Americans engaged in pitched battles in
an attempt to regain control of a culture which they felt to be
slipping away from them, their British brothers, knowing only
too well that their beliefs had already been displaced at the
centre of culture, retired to the Lake District to pursue an
essentially non-controversialist piety in the Keswick Convention, focusing attention on personal holiness and quietly ignoring both socio-political concerns and uncomfortable questions
concerning the doctrinal purity of the denominations to which
they belonged. At Keswick one met with believers of like mind
under a banner which proclaimed 'All One In Christ Jesus' and
the tranquillity of such a setting was about as far removed from
the vulgar conflicts of noisy Americans as could be imagined.

At the same time, voices were heard within British Evangelicalism calling for a reassessment of modern thought. A
volume edited by T. Guy Rogers appeared in 1923 which
advocated what was called *Liberal Evangelicalism*. Rogers explained that while he and his fellow writers wished to identify
with the tradition begun during the eighteenth-century Revival, the 'environment' in which they felt at home was that of
'the modern world with its historical method, its philosophy
of personality, and its scientific view of the universe'

(Rogers:1923,v). Here were men who wished to dissent from the tactics of opposition and withdrawal from the modern world. Their evaluation of contemporary thought was overwhelmingly positive and they were severely critical of the received Evangelical tradition. They acknowledged the importance of the traditional soteriological emphasis but warned that 'though evangelicalism can give birth to children, she cannot always keep them at her side' (Ibid:26). Tenacious resistance to the new learning, which had been perversely praised as 'loyalty to the old paths', had resulted in the loss of multitudes of young people from Evangelicalism and this 'process of attrition' would continue 'so long as the fatal fear that knowledge can destroy truth retains its power' (Ibid:26).

Some Liberal Evangelicals went as far as to grant modern thought normative status. The 'new knowledge', said V.F. Storr, 'is a fresh revelation from God' and the findings of modern biblical scholarship must 'be attributed to the illumination of that Spirit of Truth whom Christ promised as our guide into all truth' (Ibid:81–2). The extent to which these writers were willing to accommodate Evangelicalism to modern thought is seen in E.A. Burroughs' acknowledgement that their approach to the theological task involved a 'frank subjectivity' in which they did not shrink from 'judging God by ourselves'. There is a sense, said Burroughs, in which man must always be the measure of all things, 'even of God' (Ibid:52–3). Evangelical belief is here treading the path identified by Friedrich Schleiermacher as theology is reduced to anthropology.

The majority of British Evangelicals in the 1920s were unlikely to heed the call to embrace Liberalism. Many suspected that T. Guy Rogers and his friends were advocating not merely an accommodation to modern thought so much as capitulation to it. E.J. Poole-Connor, who was one of the few men to support the American Fundamentalists, said that the phrase 'Liberal Evangelicalism' involved a logical contradiction and that those who used it were disguising their own loss of faith (Poole- Connor:1966,268). J. Russell Howden, in a 1925 volume entitled *Evangelicalism*, referred to the postwar confusion and division within the movement as the result of the split between 'Liberals' and 'Conservatives'. The contributors to this book were clearly engaged in a line-holding exercise, yet it contains indications that, had they not been driven onto the defensive by the uncritical advocacy of modern thought on the part of the Liberal Evangelicals, they might have dealt with the relationship between Evangelical belief and contemporary scholarship in a constructive and creative manner. For example, G.T. Manley, who was unwilling to argue for the complete inerrancy of the Bible, wrote that the peculiar difficulty in forming a right estimate of modern criticism did not lie in any objection to critical scholarship *per se*, but in the 'close connection . . . between a rationalistic philosophy and the critical conclusions which it has brought into being' (Howdon, ed.:1925,146). While Evangelicals would continue to insist on the divine inspiration of the early chapters of Genesis, Manley said, they should also gladly welcome each new discovery of science as a contribution toward the correct interpretation of the biblical account of creation (Ibid:153). This stance, which is not dissimilar to the critical appropriation of modern thought which we noted earlier on the part of the Scottish theologians Orr and Denney, was sadly not developed further at this time.

It is clear that the Evangelical movement as a whole faced a very considerable crisis in the first three decades of this century. In 1923 E.W. Barnes observed that for the previous fifty years Evangelicalism had been losing ground because, in its failure to address the issues raised by the revolutionary changes in human thought which had occurred during this period, the movement seemed to bear the label of another age. By staking its whole case on the defence of a system 'based explicitly on the past', Barnes said, it doomed itself to irrelevance in the eyes of educated men and women (Rogers, ed.:1923,71–2). Whatever criticisms may be levelled at the Liberal Evangelicals, their awareness of contemporary realities prompted a genuine concern for the effective communication of the Christian faith in a world which, post-Nietzsche and post-Einstein, had changed beyond recognition from the era in which Evangelicalism had been born and flourished. For them the refashioning of the tradition was imperative if it was to survive and stand a chance of claiming the allegiance of thinking young people in the twentieth century.

Conservative Evangelicals might respond that the growth of the Inter-Varsity Fellowship in this period showed that their theological response to modernity was perfectly capable of winning the allegiance of undergraduates in British universities. By contrast, the Student Christian Movement, which adopted a policy of dialogue and accommodation with modern culture, went into decline during the inter-war years. A case can indeed be made, sociologically as well as missiologically, to support this claim and the strength of Evangelical witness among British students throughout the twentieth century has been truly remarkable. Nonetheless, the *form* of piety encouraged at this time provides evidence of a general retreat from involvement in social and cultural concerns and the acceptance of the split between the private world, where faith operates, and the public realm, controlled by ideas hostile to religion.

In 1936 the Inter-Varsity Fellowship published a small book by Howard Guinness with the title *SACRIFICE: A Challenge to Christian Youth*. By 1957 it had gone through four editions and had been reprinted no less than sixteen times. The success of the book is not difficult to understand; it contained a simple and direct challenge to Christian discipleship which left the reader with no doubts about the radical nature of the call of Christ. Indeed, at some points Guinness anticipates the call to a 'simple life-style' that has been a feature of more recent Evangelical writing. Life, he says, has become far too easy and too much removed from the simplicity of Christ (Guinness: 1950,14). Devotional writing of this kind, based on a Keswick view of sanctification, was capable of exerting immense influence on young lives and of inspiring people in self-sacrificial missionary labours. And yet, there is nothing here about the problems and challenges of a culture which no longer knows the language used in this booklet. When the author does mention the intellectual realm, he warns his student readers that to 'assimilate mental poison is far more dangerous than to take physical poison'. With regard to their academic work, students are told that if there is anything which cannot be named as Christ's, 'it would be better dropped' (Ibid:38–9). Clearly, this approach is the antithesis of the accommodationist strategy of the SCM, but it is easy to see how such attempts to place certain aspects of human learning off limits to young converts might lead to disaster when the flood of modern knowledge began to pour through some breach in the ghetto walls.

This was then something of a 'dark age' in the story we are relating. E.J. Poole-Connor surveyed the inter-war period and spoke of the 'defeat of Evangelicalism in this country'. Yet in the early 1930s a movement of spiritual revival occurred in Port Talbot in South Wales. The correspondent of a local newspaper described this area as one of the most difficult imaginable for Christian evangelism: 'sandy wastes and dreary, crowded houses,' he wrote, 'convey a sense of desolation, almost of hopelessness' (Murray:1982,224). It had been estimated that less than ten per cent of the population attended church and there was a complete indifference to religion among the respectable working class. Yet in 1931 a dramatic increase was recorded in the membership of the Presbyterian Forward Movement church in Sandfields; 223 members were added in two years and the majority of these were described as being 'from the world'. This movement was clearly against the dominant trends in the history of British religion in this period. It had wider significance, however, since the man at the centre of the revival was soon to become an Evangelical leader of considerable importance who, when he succeeded G. Campbell Morgan at London's Westminster Chapel after the Second World War, exerted a profound influence on Evangelicalism as a whole.

The man in question was Dr David Martyn Lloyd-Jones who had abandoned a brilliant medical career in Harley Street because, as he put it, 'I became more interested in people than in their diseases'. Deeply read in the English Puritans and in the works of Jonathan Edwards, as well as in more recent theologians like P.T. Forsyth, Lloyd-Jones was to challenge the intellectual and spiritual shallowness of much contemporary Evangelicalism and, through an outstanding preaching ministry in central London, was a major influence in the post-war resurgence of Evangelical religion.

We shall be returning to Lloyd-Jones later; I have cited his pre-Second-World-War ministry here as an illustration of the fact that while the world-transformative tradition of Evangelicalism may be described as 'underground' in this period, that term can be applied to living seeds as well as to corpses.

Harringay to Lausanne

In the years immediately following the Second World War there were a number of indications that a resurgence of British Evangelical Christianity might be occurring. The War, like the earlier conflict in 1914–18, offered the opportunity of looking afresh at life and its purpose. Albert Camus wrote that 'the philosophy of the age of enlightenment finally led to the Europe of the black-out' (Camus:1971,201). In less than half a century Europe had twice been devastated by conflicts more terrible than any known to history and the confident claims of those who had predicted a golden age as the result of humankind's emancipation from the juvenile superstitions of religion now appeared very hollow. At the same time, Christians were compelled to engage in critical self-examination. The absolute nature of the decline of institutional religion in Britain was an inescapable reality and Christians were bound to reflect on the challenges to faith in the context of what appeared to be an increasingly secular culture. It could be argued that the War finally severed the Evangelical movement from the memory of its Victorian phase and thus liberated it from the burden of that past ascendency, enabling it to confront the challenge of evangelizing a non-Christian society. In an age when it was obvious to all but the most blinkered that Christendom was a thing of the past, Evangelical energies could be directed away from the negative tasks associated with shoring up the remnants of the *Corpus Christianum* toward the positive work of bearing witness to Christ in a Europe committed to the work of reconstruction.

There is evidence that Evangelical activities in the universities were especially fruitful in the post-war period. The Inter-Varsity Fellowship began to shed its narrowly pietistic image and entered a new phase marked by considerable growth. One Oxford don bemoaned the fact that 'those ranting fundamentalists, those schoolboys in the OICCU, have only to offer tea and some buns, and a Bible-punching evangelist, and they get crowded out!' (Hopkinson:1983,65). Moreover, the beginning of Lloyd-Jones' long and immensely influential ministry at Westminster Chapel was paralleled in Anglican Evangelical circles by the appearance of a new generation of leaders who, not having been personally involved in the internecine struggles of the 1920s, were able to give the party new direction. John Stott, who has been called 'one of the most influential figures in the Christian world' (Hastings:1986,455), began his crucially important work as Rector of All Souls in central London in 1950.

Thus, by the time the American evangelist Billy Graham arrived in Britain to conduct his three-month long 'Greater London Crusade' in 1954, something of an Evangelical resurgence was already underway. Graham's meetings in the Harringay Arena, with closing rallies at Wembley Stadium and the White City Stadium, drew an aggregate attendance of 185,000 people and attracted immense publicity. They also marked crucial turning points in the lives of many who attended them; as Hastings says, 'very many a fervent Evangelical in later years would look back on Harringay as the moment of truth' (Ibid). Thousands of young people from churches which had known decades of decline and introspection were taken to these rallies and, in the context of a Christian assembly of unimagined size and excitement, responded positively to Graham's straightforward challenge to 'decide for Christ'.

Two years after the Greater London Crusade Billy Graham was back in England, this time for a mission to the University of Cambridge. This caused a tremendous furore which was reflected in a lengthy correspondence in the pages of The Times. 'The recent increase of fundamentalism among university students,' said one contributor, 'cannot but cause concern to those whose work lies in religious education.' The writer went on to ask (in somewhat illiberal fashion) whether fundamentalism should be allowed a hearing at Cambridge. A spate of letters followed, some supporting the American evangelist's right to a fair hearing, others deploring his beliefs as (in the phrase used by Canon John L. Collins) 'an evil doctrine'. All seemed to agree on the 'growing appeal' of conservative religion. One of the most interesting letters came from the well-known Islamicist, Alfred Guillaume. He had taken the trouble to go and hear the evangelist and had been deeply impressed. He acknowledged that some of Graham's converts might later be faced with intellectual problems when 'they try to explain to themselves and others their spiritual, psychological experiences and try to relate them to the words of the Bible'. But, said Guillaume, it is the function of a teaching church to help such people. The critical analysis of the Bible was doubtless important for that teaching task, but it had little to offer the unconverted: 'Only the preaching of Christ crucified, which St Paul called foolishness, can help men in their unhappiness and pessimism.'

As we have seen, most British Evangelicals stood apart from the Fundamentalist movement in the United States in the inter-war years. A good illustration of the difference in spirit and policy is provided by Lloyd-Jones' account of a conversation he had in Canada in 1932 with the Fundamentalist leader, T.T. Shields. He told Shields that he deplored the negative slant which had come to dominate his preaching and pleaded with him to abandon his constant vituperative attacks on liberal theologians and to return to the positive preaching of the Gospel (Murray:1982,273). By the time Billy Graham arrived in Britain in the '50s, a new generation of American Evangelicals had come round to Lloyd-Jones' position and were themselves actively promoting an image designed to distance them from the militancy of their Fundamentalist fathers. Graham was himself a key figure in the moves to create what some called 'Fundamentalism with a human face'. Much to the chagrin of his early Fundamentalist backers, Billy Graham now sought active co-operation with churchmen of all shades of theological opinion. British Evangelicals were happy to welcome their American friends back to the mainstream of the movement after the unfortunate interlude of Fundamentalist bigotry. Thus, John Stott wrote to *The Times* to insist that neither he nor Billy Graham wished to have their theological position designated by a term which 'has come to be associated with extremes and extravagances and to be a synonym for obscurantism'. There was a distinction, Stott argued, between Fundamentalism and the traditional conservative view of Scripture; the latter did not involve 'a bigoted rejection of all biblical criticism' or an excessively literalist interpretation of the Bible.

This debate over Fundamentalism rumbled on throughout the '50s and '60s. Critics suggested that the suppression of the offensive title was merely a smokescreen which disguised the fact that, in its view of the Bible and its attitude toward other Christians (and especially toward those of liberal views), modern Evangelicalism was indistinguishable from Fundamentalism. Or, as one more recent observer has put it, Evangelicals are simply 'fundamentalists with good manners'. J.I. Packer's book *Fundamentalism and the Word of God* seemed to lend support to this view. Packer accepted the dictionary definition of Fundamentalism as the 'maintenance, in opposition to modernism, of traditional orthodox beliefs such as the inerrancy of Scripture and literal acceptance of the creeds . . .' and said that *in this sense* British Evangelicals should not hesitate to admit themselves to be Fundamentalists (Packer:1958,29). Fundamentalism had been 'Evangelicalism at something less than its best' and the battles between conservatives and modernists in the United States in the earlier part of the century had 'not been a happy chapter in the history of Evangelicalism' (Ibid:31–2). Nonetheless, 'Fundamentalism' was just 'a twentieth-century name for historic Evangelicalism' and those who had fought the good fight in the '20s and '30s deserved to be honoured for their witness 'at a time when a militant Liberalism threatened to sweep the historic faith away' (Ibid:38). Thus, in their basic theological convictions, and especially in their defence of the inerrancy of the Bible, the Fundamentalists were merely defending historic Christianity and their position was one which Packer wholeheartedly endorsed.

The Evangelical resurgence continued with increasing momentum throughout the 1950s. A stream of Graham converts found their way into the theological colleges and thence into the Christian ministry with the result that committed Evangelicals began to form significant groups in all the major denominations. There was also a surge in Evangelical publishing; the Inter-Varsity Press increased both the range and the depth of its books and new publishing houses appeared on the scene. The Banner of Truth Trust, for example, began republishing classics of Reformed and Puritan divinity and had considerable influence on young Evangelical ministers in the '60s. The circulation of such books, combined with the influence resulting from Martyn Lloyd-Jones' multi-faceted ministry, led to a revival of Calvin-istic theology as a new generation of pastors came to see them-selves as the heirs, not so much of the Keswick holiness tradition, but of a theological and spiritual movement which could be traced back through the eighteenth-century Revival to the English Puritans and the Reformers. Thus many factors combined to produce a situation in which Evangelical Christi-anity, following at least half a century of disorderly retreat, recovered what Hastings describes as 'a major and initiating role in English religion' (Hastings:1986,458).

It is extremely important, however, to keep in mind the wider cultural context in which this revival of Evangelicalism was occurring. On the opening night of his Greater London Crusade in March, 1954, Billy Graham had predicted that within five years Britain would be witnessing 'a spiritual awakening such as you have not seen since the days of Wesley' (Ibid:454). This confident prophecy was not fulfilled. Indeed, by the end of the '60s, Evangelicals were themselves beginning to doubt the effectiveness of Graham's 'Crusade' style evan-gelism as a means of reaching the great bulk of the British population, which remained as impervious to Christian preaching as ever. The Evangelical Alliance published the report of a Commission it had set up to investigate the spiritual state of Britain and recommend the most fruitful methods of bearing witness in a secular culture. The Commission under-took detailed research and came to the conclusion that, what-ever may have been its value in reviving and encouraging the Evangelical sub-culture, Crusade evangelism on the Billy Graham model had made absolutely minimal impact on the surrounding world. The research revealed that, in the country at large, ministers and church-members felt little confidence in this method. The report, entitled *On The Other Side*, urged Evangelicals to recognize the huge cultural gap between their churches and the modern world and concluded that, given the sub-cultural nature of the Evangelical worldview, it was doubtful whether many secular contemporaries 'can be taken from a position of complete ignorance to full faith in Christ within the compass of one rally' (Evangelical Alliance: 1968a,168). An obvious corollary of this was the frank recognition that most of the Graham converts whose profession of faith lasted beyond the immediate response to the evangelist's 'appeal' were people with 'a church background or association'. In the context of the 1960s, said the Commission, Christian preaching must take seriously the task of apologetics and it must deal with the fundamental question of God before it speaks about Christ. *On The Other Side* was an important volume which attempted to take very seriously the challenge of a secular culture and refused to mistake the resurgence of Evangelicalism for a widespread revival of religion in modern Britain.

Sociological studies of Crusade style evangelism have confirmed the findings of the Evangelical Alliance Commission. Steve Bruce undertook research which led to the conclusion that most conversions to 'born again' Christianity are 'not moves from one universe to another but rather a "change of heart" within a universe'. This is not to say that people with a thoroughly secular cast of mind are *never* converted to Christianity by such evangelism, but Bruce was correct when he said that the vast majority of converts were actually committing themselves to 'a set of propositions about the world with which they have long been acquainted' (Bruce:1982,110–12).

It should be sobering for Evangelicals to reflect that such observations as these simply echo the analysis which Charles Dickens made of the ineffectiveness of their predecessors' attempts to reach the masses beyond the confines of middle-class religiosity a century earlier.

By the end of the '60s Evangelicals began to revise their thinking and tactics as the realities of the modern world came to impinge upon them more closely. In 1968 the Inter-Varsity Press published Francis Schaeffer's book *Escape From Reason* followed, two years later, by Hans Rookmaaker's *Modern Art and the Death of a Culture*. Here were Evangelical authors who were well aware of the importance of apologetics, or what Schaeffer called 'pre-evangelism', if the Gospel message were ever to be heard by the majority in the population who had no prior acquaintance with the language and thought of the religious sub-culture. In order to reach intellectuals and the working class, both groups, Schaeffer said, 'right outside our middle-class churches', Evangelicals would need to 'do a great deal of heart-searching as to how we may speak what is eternal into a changing historical situation' (Schaeffer:1968,93). Confronted with the counter-cultural movements of the '60s, Schaeffer recognized that many Christians were facing growing problems in speaking to their own children, let alone other people's:

> Through reading and education and the whole modern cultural bombardment of mass media, even today's middle-class children are becoming thoroughly twentieth-century in outlook. In crucial areas many Christian parents, ministers and teachers are as out of touch with many of the children of the church, and the majority of those outside, as though they were speaking a foreign language (Ibid:94).

Under the influence of such books younger Evangelicals now began to explore the meaning of modern culture. Art, drama, cinema, all of which had previously been viewed as, at best, peripheral, or more usually, as taboo, now became essential to the proper understanding of the world within which the Christian was called to witness. At the same time, Evangelicalism began to turn from a preoccupation with the salvation of individuals toward a more comprehensive view of its mission and the outworking of the confession of the Lordship of Christ in every aspect of cultural life.

Not all Evangelicals were happy with these trends. In 1952 Lloyd-Jones had issued a vigorous call to maintain the Evangelical faith in the face of pressures to modify or compromise it and had stated that this would involve a resolute refusal 'to surrender any single part of what is vital to the full evangelical faith as recorded in the Holy Scriptures' (Lloyd-Jones:1952,4). If this policy should attract charges of intolerance, then Christians should regard this as a *compliment*. Lloyd-Jones, whose influence was considerable, had done much to encourage a return to the theology of the Reformers and Puritans with the result that not only was there a renewed interest in doctrine, but the Puritan ideal of a pure church became the subject of much discussion. A number of Evangelicals actually seceded from the Anglican Church, including Herbert Carson who described how, listening to Lloyd-Jones speaking at a meeting to commemorate the 'Great Ejection' of 1662, he felt his own position within Anglicanism to be impossible: 'If the Puritans were right – and I believed they were – then how could I reconcile my own continuance in the ministry of the established church?' (Carson:1969,20). Thus, up to 1966 the path of secession from denominations which tolerated unbiblical teaching and the formation of a church founded unequivocally upon an Evangelical confession of faith was the subject of animated debate within the movement as a whole.

In October of 1966 that debate was brought to a juddering halt. The Evangelical Alliance invited Lloyd-Jones to address its National Assembly in the Central Hall, Westminster on the subject of the doctrine of the church. He did so and used the occasion to expound views for which he was already well known: ecumenism based on a minimalist approach to Christian doctrine was an abomination; Evangelicals who remained in denominations which tolerated heresy were recognizing the ministry of men 'who denied their Lord'; Evangelicals must join together to honour the truth and form an ecclesiastical alliance on the basis of a common faith and doctrine. At the close of this address John Stott, who was in the chair, rose to dissent from Lloyd-Jones' position. The option of sectarian withdrawal, Stott said, could not be justified on either biblical or historical grounds.

Here, clearly, was the parting of the ways. This public disagreement between the two outstanding post-war leaders of Evangelicalism probably accelerated a process of rethinking already underway among Anglicans. The focal point of this new thinking was the National Evangelical Anglican Congress (NEAC) held at Keele University in April 1967. Over a thousand people attended this Congress and the resultant 'Keele Statement', which committed Evangelicals to social concern, ecumenical activity as loyal members of the Church of England, and a determination to relate the Gospel meaningfully to the modern world, was an important landmark in the history of the movement. Three months after the Congress at Keele, representatives of the Anglican Evangelical Group Movement, which had been the organ of the Liberal Evangelical tradition we noted earlier, met in Oxford and decided to terminate the existence of their organization. To a significant degree, the agenda of Liberal Evangelicalism had been adopted at the Keele Congress.

One other significant feature of the 1960s must be noted. In 1964 Michael Harper, a Stott curate at All Souls, London, resigned his position there and founded the Fountain Trust, an organization dedicated to the promotion of the Charismatic movement. Yet another potent ingredient was added to the cocktail of contemporary Evangelicalism.

If the '60s had seen a resurgent Evangelicalism divided in its reaction to the realities of the modern world, the '70s were to bring an even more astonishing transformation. Throughout its history, even in what we have called the 'dark age', Evangelicalism continued to stress the importance of missions and provided personnel and financial backing for a host of organizations working to spread the Gospel to every corner of the globe. John Kent has made the provocative suggestion that continued enthusiasm for missionary work in exotic locations can be interpreted as 'a flight from the problems of being religious in a sophisticated Western society' (Kent:1978,203). However that may be, the preaching of the missionaries had been extraordinarily fruitful, so that in South America, Asia and, above all, in sub-Saharan Africa, young churches were growing at an astonishing rate. These Third World churches had long since reached maturity and were asserting their independence both organizationally and theologically. It was from this source that the most searching questions now began to be raised concerning Evangelicalism's faithfulness to the Gospel. Theologians from the burgeoning churches in Africa and Latin America acknowledged their indebtedness to western Christianity but asked how it was that the missionary movement had allowed itself to be led into illicit alliances with colonialism in the nineteenth century, and western consumerism in the twentieth. Issues like these made the internal disagreements of British Evangelicalism pale into insignificance, yet they struck deep chords in the hearts of many younger Evangelicals who, having already been challenged on just such subjects by the radical counter-cultural movements of the '60s, were ready to listen to the questions coming from the Third World with considerable sympathy.

The issues in this debate came into clear focus at the Lausanne Congress on World Evangelization in 1974. This international assembly of 2,700 people, including almost every known leader in the Evangelical movement worldwide, was without doubt a watershed in the history of modern Evangelical religion. Prior to the Lausanne Congress Billy Graham declared that it would be a meeting 'of those totally committed to the evangelical position as we understand it'. People who held 'liberal or controversial positions', he said, had not been invited. In other words, the Graham organization, which funded the Congress to the tune of well over two million dollars, planned the meeting in such a way that there would be no departure from the chosen agenda and no rocking of the Evangelical boat. The organizers were evidently unprepared for the storms about to break over their heads and one can only assume that they had not done their homework with regard to some of those invited to present keynote addresses to the Congress.

Adrian Hastings describes John Stott as Lausanne's 'principal theoretician' and credits him with responsibility for the direction taken by the Congress (Hastings:1986,616). Stott's role was extremely important but Hastings fails to recognize that the speakers who set the Congress alight and placed new questions on the Evangelical agenda spoke with neither American nor English public-school accents, but with the voices of people who had grown up on the receiving end of western missionary work in Africa and South America. In fact, Stott's role appears to have been that of a ringmaster, attempting to hold the balance between astonished Americans, who had come to Europe assuming that the delegates would simply fall into line with their plans to complete the evangelization of

the world by the greater use of modern technology, and Third
World theologians who insisted on rewriting the agenda with
their demands for a fundamental rethink about the basis and
nature of the Christian mission.

The volume containing the papers delivered at Lausanne is
an extraordinarily rich resource for the understanding of this
critical moment in Evangelical history. The papers prepared
by keynote speakers were circulated to participants in advance
of the Congress and at Lausanne the authors responded to
questions raised by correspondents. Samuel Escobar's paper
on 'Evangelism and Man's Search for Freedom, Justice and
Fulfillment' began by pointing out that Evangelicals had
opposed the violence of revolution but not the violence of war:

> They condemn the totalitarianism of the left but not that of the right;
> they speak openly in favor of Israel, but very seldom speak or do
> anything about the Palestinian refugees; they condemn all the sins
> that well-behaved middle-class people condemn but say nothing
> about exploitation, intrigue, and dirty political maneuvering done by
> the great multi-national corporations around the world (Douglas,
> ed.:1975,304).

Escobar identified himself unreservedly with the concern of
the Congress for effective evangelism, but insisted that this did
not amount to discovering ways of merely increasing the
number of people professing conversion. The *quality* of converts
and the integrity and faithfulness of the life of the Christian
community were essential considerations. Unfortunately,
western Christianity had become almost indistinguishable
from a way of life which seemed to have little in common with
the radical discipleship found on the pages of the New Testament and had, in consequence, lost the ability to speak prophetically to the modern world. Third World believers,
Escobar said, expected from their brothers in the West 'a word
of identification with demands for justice in international
trade, for a modification of the patterns of affluence and waste
. . . for a criticism of corruption in the arms race and in the
almost omnipotent maneuverings of international intelligence
agencies' (Ibid:316).

René Padilla's paper entitled 'Evangelism and the World'
contained a masterly survey of the biblical doctrine of the

church in the world which paralleled Escobar's material at a number of points. In western Christianity, Padilla said, the goals and methods of evangelism have been shaped by the dominant secular ideology of consumerism rather than by the principles enunciated within the Bible. Modern culture-Christianity is a religion tailor-made for consumer society since it allows secular people to believe they may have the comfort and assurance offered by the Gospel without requiring them to face the costly demands of discipleship. Attacking the preoccupation of Evangelicals with the purely quantitative growth of the church, Padilla insisted that statistics on 'how many souls die without Christ every minute' were irrelevant if 'they do not take into account how many of those who die, die victims of hunger' (Ibid:131).

These new voices from the Third World churches challenged the claims of western Christianity to have exported the pure Gospel of Christ. Rather, the Gospel had reached Africa and Latin America in a cultural wrapper and men like Escobar and Padilla insisted that, while Christians in their poor and exploited lands recognized and treasured the gift of the Gospel, they had every right to strip away the extraneous wrapper and consign it to the wastebin. These searching analyses placed a whole series of demanding issues firmly on the Evangelical agenda: henceforth questions concerning the Gospel and culture, the relationship between preaching and social justice, and the appropriate Christian response to the secularized culture of the western world would loom large among Evangelical theologians.

The Lausanne Covenant, drafted during the Congress and affirmed by participants at its close, reflected the extent to which the Evangelical community was already willing to respond positively to the critical voices to which it had listened. A year after the Congress René Padilla edited a volume in which various authors expounded the Covenant chapter by chapter. The title encapsulated the momentous changes set in motion at Lausanne. It was called *The New Face of Evangelicalism* (Padilla, ed.:1976).

A stream of publications now appeared which were dedicated to rediscovering and redefining Evangelicalism's social

conscience. The most radical contribution came from the
United States. Ronald Sider's *Rich Christians in an Age of Hun-*
ger: A Biblical Study was widely read and sparked passionate
debates concerning economic justice and the style of life appropriate to those who claimed to be the followers of Jesus of
Nazareth in a world where millions of people were starving to
death. One chapter in this book was headed by the question 'Is
God A Marxist?' Sider did not give a positive answer, but he
did argue that the Almighty 'sides with the poor because he
disapproves of extremes of wealth and poverty' (Sider:
1977,84). The effect of all this within a constituency which for
half a century had identified itself as 'conservative' can well
be imagined. The year which saw the publication of Sider's
book also witnessed the launching of the new journal *Third*
Way devoted to the discussion of socio-political issues and the
encouragement of a serious, critical Evangelical engagement
with modern culture.

New day or false dawn?

Viewed within the broad historical perspectives of this book,
the 1970s seemed to mark a new day of opportunity for British
Evangelicalism. This decade provided an opportunity to recover the world-transformative character of the evangelical
tradition and to face up to the immense challenges posed by
modernity. The Lausanne Congress reminded Evangelicals of
the social dimensions of their faith in the context of a tragically
divided world and it stimulated critical theological reflection
on the extent to which inherited traditions of belief and practice had been influenced by the secular culture of the West.
Writing about the Lausanne Covenant, René Padilla observed
that it was permeated by a note of repentance. It expressed, he
said, a determination to ensure that evangelism should never
again be divorced from social responsibility, discipleship and
church renewal. Evangelicals at Lausanne renounced evangelism as mere 'ecclesiocentric activism' and affirmed instead that
it is 'God's means of placing the totality of life under the
lordship of Jesus Christ' (Padilla:1976,14). The Congress also

made the international character of the Evangelical family clearly visible and highlighted the reality of the growth and theological vitality of churches in the non-western world.

Within the United Kingdom Evangelicalism was now attracting the attention of theologians and scholars anxious to defend the liberal consensus of institutional Christianity. For example, James Barr noted that 'persons who hold markedly conservative views' were now to be found in growing numbers teaching biblical or theological studies in academic posts and he concluded that, so far as opportunities in higher education were concerned, 'the secularized world has proved to be a not unfavourable environment for the conservative evangelical' (Barr:1978,103). Barr's detailed studies of what he insisted on calling 'Fundamentalism' included a volume bearing the provocative title *Escaping From Fundamentalism* (Barr:1984). His books contained evidence that, as he put it, the revival of Evangelicalism was 'an extremely irritating phenomenon' (Barr:1978,336). Having earlier argued *against* Fundamentalists that the concept of heresy has little meaning in the modern world, he nonetheless warned mainline churches against being 'weakly welcoming and appeasing' to the new, open breed of Evangelicals, with their more positive approach toward scholarship. It is questionable, Barr said, how far mainline Christians can 'recognize fundamentalist attitudes, doctrines and interpretations as coming within the range that is acceptable in the church' (Barr:1978,344). There is deep irony here; Barr's identification of 'Fundamentalism' as the one heresy which must be excluded from the modern church reminds one irresistibly of the exclusivism with which the Fundamentalist movement itself has often been charged.

By the close of the 1970s then, Evangelicalism seemed to be ready to acknowledge the failings of the past, to throw off unbiblical accretions which had weakened its witness in the modern world, and to enter a new phase in which, in fellowship with the worldwide church, it might address the serious missiological challenges facing it in an era of cultural crisis and growing despair. However, not everyone agreed that the events we have described marked the arrival of a new day; for some people they were best described as a false dawn.

Following the Second Evangelical Anglican Congress held at
Nottingham University in April, 1977, reports appeared in
the Christian press indicating that many delegates went home
with a deepening sense of identity crisis, wondering what it
now meant to be 'Evangelical'. Some of these people hank-
ered after the old certainties and regretted the new openness,
others began to ask how they might justify perpetuating a
separate and distinctive Evangelical tradition. The Congress
had pushed the critical reassessment of received Evangelical
traditions to a new level, insisting that the time had come to
engage in a radical re-examination of traditional views
which, instead of merely scratching the surface, would actually expose the roots of the belief-system. John Stott welcomed evidence of repentance for 'past pietism' but argued
that Evangelicals had not yet progressed far enough along the
new paths. There was need to review the most cherished
theological convictions since 'theological reformulation is indispensable' (Stott:1977,17). One of the most cherished of
theological convictions concerned the authority of the Bible
and in this key area of doctrine the Nottingham Congress was
told that unless proper recognition was granted to the fact
that both the biblical text and the modern reader are condi-
tioned by specific cultural contexts, there would be grounds
to suspect that, however loudly Evangelicals declared their
subjection to the Bible, their real source of authority was 'a
particular evangelical tradition of biblical interpretation, pre-
served in what is sometimes unkindly described as a ghetto
community' (Ibid:93). This was heady stuff and while some
began to hear alarm bells ringing, others noticed a growing
theological convergence between Evangelicals and other
streams of Christian tradition.

Outside the Anglican constituency one voice which
sounded a very clear alarm at the new developments was that
of Dr Martyn Lloyd-Jones. The minister of Westminster
Chapel was certainly one of the most important of modern
Evangelical leaders. His influence was diffused throughout
the movement and can often be detected in unlikely places; he
has been listed alongside Stott, David Watson, Colin Buchanan
and Jim Packer when discussing the most important models

for Evangelical *Anglicans* between 1960 and 1980. In addition, some significant leaders within the Charismatic movement have claimed him as their mentor. Lloyd-Jones had constantly insisted that Evangelicals needed to rediscover both the doctrinal heritage of Protestantism and the eighteenth-century stress on religious experience as a directly supernatural phenomenon. After reading the works of the American theologian B.B. Warfield during a visit to Canada in 1932 he had become convinced of the need to supplement his powerful evangelistic preaching with doctrinal teaching which would contribute toward the 'defence of the Faith against modern error' (Murray:1982,286). Consequently, throughout the post-war period Lloyd-Jones sought to lead Evangelicals in the direction of a thorough-going anti-modernism and he opposed both Stott's more open attitude toward contemporary thought and the efforts of people like Francis Schaeffer to communicate the Gospel in a form which was relevant to modern people. If there was a place for apologetics, he said, it was not in the sphere of evangelism, for here no dialogue, no point-of-contact with non-Christian thought was possible. Apologetics could simply 'buttress the faith of the believer' by showing him the falsity and inadequacy of 'every other view apart from the biblical view' (Lloyd-Jones:1964,19). Clearly this represents an emphatic 'Christ-against-modern-culture' position. To Lloyd-Jones and his followers the ferment of ideas in Evangelicalism following the Lausanne Congress looked like the twilight which precedes the arrival of darkness.

Similar contrasts in Evangelical responses to the difficult issues raised by modernity can be seen in connection with the Charismatic movement. The Nottingham Evangelical Anglican Congress had displayed a new openness toward this increasingly pervasive phenomenon. Evidence had accumulated that the ecstatic experiences claimed by charismatics had led many Anglicans to a dynamic and joyful faith and to a new boldness in witness. People like David Watson, whose York church had become a model of what neo-pentecostal renewal might achieve within the Anglican communion, were powerful advocates of charismatic views who, by their own clearly stated commitment to the Church of England and to ecumenical dialogue, disarmed critics who feared that a stress on the immediacy of the experience of the Spirit would open the flood-gates to sectarian division. Watson and Michael Harper were able to argue that the Charismatic movement was vital to the spiritual renewal of the whole church and that, rather than leading people out of institutional religion, it offered hope for the renewal of Christendom. Spiritual renewal on the charismatic model was occurring among Nonconformists and Roman Catholics and thus seemed to provide a possible path toward a unified and dynamic church. In addition, charismatic leaders argued that the experiential dimension of religion was of the utmost importance if the Christian mission was to be effective in a shattered and broken world. The Gospel, said Michael Harper, is concerned with making people *whole* and this means more than teaching them to think correctly. Maturity is not achieved by 'believing and knowing certain Scripture texts', it also requires inner healing by means of which the 'mental and emotional damage and hurt' experienced by so many people in modern society is recognized and overcome (Stott:1977:148). Given the general direction in which Anglican Evangelicalism was now moving, it is not surprising that such emphases were welcomed and that the charismatic position came to be recognized as a valid and important perspective in a movement which was turning its face toward the modern world.

By contrast, the House Church movement represented a very different charismatic response to modernity. If one stream of the Charismatic movement was contained within the channels of established denominational religion, another moved in quite different directions and, bursting out from pre-existing structures, began to flow in unpredictable patterns across the ecclesiastical landscape. This movement demonstrated the most spectacular and least noticed growth of any religious group in modern Britain, having 'developed from practically nothing in the early 1970s to an estimated membership of sixty thousand in 1980' (Brierley:1982,6). If the key word for ecumenical charismatics was 'renewal', that of the separatists was 'restoration'. For one group the coming of the Spirit promised the possibility of reform and revival *within* existing structures, for the other it heralded the advent of the restoration of a pure church which stood in almost total contrast to the archaic institutions of Christendom. For the House Churches, all previous movements of reform or revival had been *partial* recoveries of the lost pristine religion of Christ and his apostles. Only now, at the 'end of the ages' was the church recovering its true identity and full glory as, following the 'latter-day' outpouring of the Spirit, it prepared like a bride for the advent of Christ.

The teaching of the House Churches in this period has been described as a return to Fundamentalism (Walker:1985,122) and as representing a complete contrast with the secularity of modern society (Thurman:1982,13). Nonetheless, in a fragmented, disorderly and confusing world in which moral standards appeared to have been relativized to vanishing point and society faced ills so intractable that the most clear-headed rationalists despaired of their solution, the attractiveness of the Restorationist option to men and women conscious of the aridity and loneliness of modern life is not hard to appreciate. Indeed, these churches appear to be riding a tide of disillusion with modernity which has other manifestations in the contemporary world. The offer of free forgiveness and the promise of an inner healing, the warmth of a genuinely caring community in which every member matters and there is active pastoral care, the assurance that religion is more than words or abstract concepts, that its very essence involves emotion and feeling and that it reveals a realm in which secular definitions of reality are felt to be, at best, partial, at worst, diabolic deceits, the assurance that, despite one's weakness and vulnerability, there is a power available whereby one can overcome evil and live a useful and happy life – all of these features of the Restorationist churches have seemed attractive to people who despaired of finding meaning in the secular city.

It is possible to argue that the greatest threat to the gains made by resurgent Evangelicalism as a result of the Lausanne Congress came from an *external* source in the form of the emergent New Right in British politics. During the 1988 election campaign Margaret Thatcher had claimed that the Tories were 'the party of Christianity'; soon after her victory the

Prime Minister went to Edinburgh and, speaking to the assembly of the Church of Scotland, she presented her political philosophy as the logical outworking of the fundamental principles of the Bible. In the following months government ministers tripped over each other in their attempts to woo Evangelicals and it became clear that this was part of deliberate government strategy. A number of known Evangelical Christians were close to the heart of government, none more so than Brian Griffiths, head of Margaret Thatcher's Downing Street policy unit. He was disarmingly honest in arguing that, while capitalism had demonstrated beyond doubt its ability to transform society for the better and had proved its superiority over all other economic systems, it required religious legitimation. 'The crisis of capitalism', Griffiths wrote, 'is nothing less than the crisis of humanism being played out in economic life' (Griffiths:1982,29). What was needed was the replacement of the humanist ideology which had provided the major philosophical defence of capitalism, by a *theological* justification which would demonstrate the compatability of the market system with Christian morality. Christians should set about the task of severing the market economy from secular humanism and incorporating it 'within a distinctively Christian ideology' (Griffiths:1984,112).

Brian Griffiths' approach to the Bible was the antithesis of that employed in the Lausanne Covenant: Scripture supports private ownership, wealth creation and the modern competitive capital market; the Old Testament prophets identify the sins of individuals as the root cause of social ills and demand spiritual repentance rather than socio-economic reform as the remedy (Ibid:59–60). According to Griffiths, Jesus took private ownership for granted and applauded the resourcefulness of those 'who increased their wealth' (Ibid:43). The Old Testament may provide a basis for a system of political economy, but the New Testament is concerned primarily with 'the ethics of those claiming citizenship in the new koinonia and the quality of their life there' (Griffiths:1982,77–8). That is to say, the ethical teaching of Jesus and his apostles has no relevance *beyond the private sphere*. Griffiths' theological justification for capitalism involves the removal of Christ's teaching on the kingdom of God from the discussion with the assertion that its 'dimensions were spiritual and not secular'; the kingdom concerns 'the reign of God over the lives of individuals' and shows humankind's fundamental problem as 'spiritual and not political' (Griffiths:1984,44). Having thus slammed the door of the public realm shut against the ethics of Jesus, it is possible to express Christian support for Adam Smith's notion of the 'invisible hand' since, 'in a world of scarcity' competitive markets are 'superior to other practical forms of economic organisation' (Ibid:69–73).

Such blandishments from the New Right began to draw a positive response from Evangelicals. The millionaire pop-star Cliff Richard, one of Evangelicalism's greatest culture heroes, declared himself an uncritical supporter of Thatcherism and argued that a country run on Christian principles would tax all its citizens, rich and poor, at a flat rate of ten per cent. Much more disturbing for those who believed that the Lausanne Congress had marked the beginning of a quest to recover the world-transformative tradition were the indications that the Evangelical Alliance was ready to adopt Thatcherite concepts and terminology. The Alliance announced that it was joining in partnership with the government in a project designed to help the unemployed to be known as 'Evangelical Enterprise'. Moreover, this project would be partly funded through a seminar the Evangelical Alliance was holding at the Hilton Hotel on Park Lane, London on 'How To Run A Business'. Businessmen were informed that the seminar would 'show you how to run your business more profitably, how to expand it and how to get the best out of your staff'. Clearly, Brian Griffiths' hope that Evangelicalism might provide a religious ideology for market capitalism was not entirely without foundation.

History was here repeating itself since, as we have seen, nineteenth century Evangelical religion was used for ideological purposes by those who wished to preserve the social status quo. I have suggested that, whatever the short-term benefits of that move in regard to the recruitment of 'those who count', the alliance between Evanglicalism and sociopolitical conservatism may have been a major factor in the secularisation of British society. It also proved fatal for the movement itself; privatised, domesticated and rendered politically harmless by a bourgeoisie which sought ideological underpinning for its way of ordering society, Evangelicalism went into decline when the system to which it had become wedded collapsed. Socially significant religion is always liable to face pressures from those who would seek to co-opt it in the interests of particular political ideologies, whether yesterday's New Right or today's New Labour. Facing such pressures, Evangelicals would do well to listen to one of their most perceptive and effective recent apologists: in *The Church at the End of the Twentieth Century* Francis Schaeffer warned that when Christians 'make peace with the Establishment and identify with it' then '. . . the institutional church is finished' (Schaeffer:1970,99).

5

The Futures of Evangelicalism

The Evangelical tradition stemming from the Great Awakening in the eighteenth century is now two hundred years old. The previous chapters have suggested that the movement has changed over time, taking different forms, not all of which remained in touch with the world-transformative impulse which so clearly shaped the first generation of Evangelicals. We have seen that, after a period of withdrawal and decline, the 1970s witnessed a resurgent movement on the verge of recovering the social dimensions of its faith and poised to play a key role in the Christian mission at the close of the twentieth century. In this final chapter I want to identify some of the important voices to be heard within the movement at present and to suggest the nature of the challenge it faces if the promise of renewal and advance in a fragmenting world is to be realized.

Evangelical voices at the close of the twentieth century

The mainstream of modern Evangelicalism is difficult to define in any very precise and accurate manner. It consists now, as has always been the case, of a coalition of groups drawn from a wide variety of denominational (and undenominational) backgrounds. Controversial issues capable of creating divisions within the movement are relegated to the level of 'secondary' matters which should not be allowed to hinder the recognition and public expression of Evangelicals' spiritual oneness, or their active co-operation together in

evangelistic and humanitarian projects. The old debate between Calvinism and Arminianism, or different views about
baptism, church-government or spiritual gifts, or attitudes
toward the modern ecumenical movement are all examples
of issues which are relegated to the secondary level of belief.
Historically the Keswick Convention, the Inter-Varsity Fellowship, and a host of interdenominational missionary and
evangelistic organizations, have operated on precisely this
basis. The agency which can lay claim to providing the most
visible institutional expression of this broad-based Evangelical unity is the *Evangelical Alliance* which 'promotes active
co-operation among groups and individuals who share the
same fundamental beliefs'.

This constituency, with its commitment to evangelism and
social concern has attracted considerable attention from the
mass media. *The Independent* newspaper interviewed Clive
Calver, then secretary of the Evangelical Alliance, and commented that British Evangelicals were clearly 'on the move'
and determined that 'they will no longer be confined to their
narrow church-going ghettoes' (Calver:1988). The newspaper
cited evidence of the surge in conservative religion: in May
1988, 50,000 Evangelicals marched through the Cities of London and Westminster to bear public witness to the Lordship
of Christ; over 30,000 signed a petition pleading for mercy for
the Sharpeville Six which was handed in at the South African
embassy in London; while the annual 'Spring Harvest' event
for worship and teaching had grown from 2,000 participants
in 1979 to 60,000 in 1988.

We can illustrate the recent growth of the movement by
citing one specific example of local renewal in recent years. The
journal *Mainstream*, which represents a group within the
Baptist Union defined as 'baptists for life and growth', reported that since 1967 churches in London's East End, all of
which had been close to extinction, were experiencing marked
growth. Between them, these congregations, all located 'in
precisely those areas of Inner London where, at one time,
others had doubted even the very survival of any Christian
church', recorded a total of 500 new members. In a testimony
which runs directly counter to many sociological predictions

of the fate of faith in the inner city, the minister of one of these churches said,

> Ever since I was converted seventeen years ago I have always belonged to and worked in inner London churches, and I have never known what it is to be in a church that is declining. I simply do not know what it means to be in a church that is not growing in love, faith and numbers. If it can happen in the East End, why can't it happen anywhere? (Griffiths T.:1988,3)

The writer goes on to claim that the experience of these churches demonstrates that a preaching ministry which is 'unashamedly evangelical in the best conservative tradition' can result in the creation of new congregations from the dust of the inner city. Growth of this kind is paralleled elsewhere among other groups identified with this mainline Evangelical tradition and, while it does not constitute evidence of a widespread revival of religion in modern society, it does suggest that the secular city may not be nearly so inhospitable to faith as has sometimes been supposed.

There are other indications that the Evangelical mainstream has been growing in a manner that poses problems to a theory of secularization which predicts the irreversible decline of religion in modern society. The modern boom in religious publishing points to the existence of 'a huge sub-culture of belief in this country'. While many of the thousands of new religious titles published every year in Britain deal with bizarre forms of the quest for the transcendent (Paul Johnson has noted that twice as many books are published on occultism as on general science), the Evangelical sector contributes substantially to this booming market. Indeed, potentially so profitable has religious publishing become that big business has taken more than a passing interest in Evangelical publishing houses.

Of course, the critical question to be asked here concerns not simply the extent of the growth of this religious sub-culture, but the character and quality of resurgent Evangelicalism and its likely impact on the wider society and culture. As we shall see, the movement still faces some formidable problems and challenges as it prepares for the task of mission in a new millennium.

Some of these challenges can be identified when considering the recent experience of *Evangelical Anglicans*. We have

already described the impact of the National Evangelical
Anglican Congresses at Keele and Nottingham. In April 1988,
three thousand Anglican Evangelicals met at Caister in Norfolk for a third Congress (or, as it was actually called, a 'celebration'). The Archbishop of Canterbury, Robert Runcie, was
invited to address this huge assembly and noted that this
invitation itself represented a greater change in the Evangelical
movement than many younger people present might realize.
He identified the Keele Congress twenty years earlier as the
catalyst which had brought about far-reaching changes among
Evangelicals, causing them to affirm without apology or hesi-
tation the *Anglican* character of their evangelicalism and creating among them a greater openness to other traditions within
the Church of England. The Archbishop recognized that much
of the vigour in modern Anglicanism was due to the Evangelical resurgence and he made generous acknowledgement of his
hosts' 'faithful and imaginative witness to the Gospel' (Runcie:
1988,15). This third Congress appeared to mark the continued
advance of Evangelicals within the national church; numerical
growth was still evident, the Evangelical theological colleges
continued to produce a stream of candidates for ordination,
the number of Evangelicals on the episcopal bench had increased, and the valuable contribution made by Evangelicals
to the Church of England now received public praise from the
Primate.

However, there were indications that, at the very moment
at which Evangelicalism appeared poised to become the dominant influence within contemporary Anglicanism, the identity
crisis we noted in the previous chapter was becoming more
acute than ever. Prior to the Caister Congress a prominent
Evangelical leader voiced his anxiety that Anglican Evangelicals were less obviously 'Gospel people' than was once the
case. The *Church of England Newspaper* carried an article with a
headline posing the question, 'End of Evangelicalism?' The
time had come, the writer argued, to recognize that exclusive
parties within the church, however necessary and valuable
their witness at particular junctures of history, indicated a
disruption of the Church which was to be lamented. Evangelicalism had fulfilled its historical purpose and the future lay

with those committed to ecumenical renewal and restoration through which 'all of God's Church' would be enabled to 'worship and love together'. Here was the beginning of what was later to be called 'Post-Evangelicalism'.

Implicit within this argument was a summons to enter into fraternal dialogue with Anglo-Catholics and Liberals within the Church of England. In fact, the old hostility toward Anglo-Catholicism had already been replaced by a new spirit of co-operation and dialogue. Furthermore, just prior to the meetings at Caister a book was published bearing the title *Essentials: A Liberal-Evangelical Dialogue*. The Liberal scholar and historian David Edwards offered a series of critical essays on John Stott's published works, to which the Evangelical leader then responded point by point. Edwards was fulsome in his praise of the Evangelical movement in general and of Stott's leadership in particular. His purpose was to try and convince Evangelicals that certain beliefs which they had always treated as 'essentials' were really nothing of the kind. Thus, belief in biblical inerrancy, the traditional doctrine of the atonement, and insistence on the literal truth of the miracle stories in the gospels, were actually a handicap to the communication of the Gospel in the modern world and if only Evangelicals would treat these ideas as 'optional' they would discover that their witness would become 'far more intelligible, meaningful and credible' (Edwards:1988,31). Stott welcomed the dialogue but politely declined the invitation to reclassify the Evangelical 'essentials'. He argued, with considerable plausibility, that the experience of Evangelicals throughout the post-war period did not confirm Edwards' view that the Bible must be systematically reinterpreted in line with the presuppositions of a secular worldview before it can be communicated effectively in the modern world. Nonetheless, Stott made it clear that the position which he defended represented what was necessary 'to be an Evangelical in particular, not a Christian in general'. In this way Edwards' Liberalism was granted the status of a possible Christian viewpoint. Stott indicated that his concern was 'to define and justify our distinctives and not to disenfranchise you or anybody else' (Ibid:332). Thus, while retaining his view of the Evangelical 'essentials' intact and rejecting the details of the Liberal position, Stott's approach involved an acceptance of theological pluralism within the church.

Soon after the Caister Congress John Stott appeared to retreat from the pluralism he had advocated in discussion with David Edwards. 'It is with self-confessed liberals in the Church of England,' he wrote, 'that we have the greatest difficulty and divergence.' Denials of the 'unique incarnation and bodily resurrection of Jesus Christ' he said, are at complete variance with Scripture and with nineteen centuries of Christian tradition and 'have no place in the Church of England' (Stott: 1988b,10).

Yet if John Stott hesitated to pass through the door which he had helped to open, some who now found themselves in positions of leadership within a comprehensive church were willing and eager to do so. George Carey, then Bishop of Bath and Wells, confessed that he owed his own soul to Evangelicalism, yet said that while his heart identified with 'the evangelical love of Jesus and a deep devotion to the biblical tradition', his head could not go along with received evangelical teaching (Carey:1988,269). Carey's encounter with Liberalism had led him to the conviction that, far from being the 'cuckoo in the nest' (as his Evangelical colleagues viewed it), it is 'a creative and constructive element for exploring theology today'. Liberal biblical scholarship, instead of being destructive of spirituality, had led to a deepening of our knowledge of God and the Bible and, Carey claimed, critical commentaries on Scripture are far more enlightening than 'the safe and filleted ones that come from pedigree evangelical publishing companies'. Unless Anglican Evangelicals recognized such facts, Carey said, they would merely perpetuate a situation in which there is 'a constant drain of good men and women who have found evangelicalism too constricting intellectually, too narrow academically and too stifling spiritually' (Ibid:270).

These statements surely remind us of the debate between Conservative and Liberal Evangelicals earlier in the century. Yet if George Carey was concerned that Anglican Evangelicalism was losing its hold on people who desired some kind of accommodation with Liberalism, at the opposite end of the spectrum there was a strong pull toward a much more conservative position. Indeed, in the years since Caister, as John Stott's influential leadership role has declined and many Anglicans became post-Evangelical, a new conservative movement opposing theological pluralism and insisting on the normative status of Evangelical doctrine has become strong and influential. This has resulted in tensions which are serious enough to lead one observer to warn that Anglican Evangelicalism may once again be about to disintegrate at a crucial moment (Saward:1995,41).

If what I have called 'mainstream' Evangelicals and the Anglican group provide the first two voices to be heard today, the third is that of Evangelicals committed to *Reformed* theology. We have noticed the revival of Calvinism in England in the 1960s as the result of Lloyd-Jones' ministry and the founding of the Banner of Truth publishing house. The rediscovery of Puritan theology and the realization that many of the earliest Evangelicals were Calvinists prompted a return to the most solid traditions of Protestant divinity. A doctrinal revival of this kind was capable of placing considerable strains on the unity of the Evangelical movement. Thus, for a time the Christian Union in Cambridge University was sharply polarized by the appearance of a strongly Calvinist group of students who criticized long-established views on evangelism, conversion and the Christian life as *departures* from historic Evangelicalism. Revivalist techniques and what came to be viewed as a man-centred Gospel were now seen as an aberration and Evangelicals were summoned to return to their roots by means of a recovery of the doctrinal Christianity of the reformers and the experiential divinity of the English Puritans. Many Evangelicals, already conscious of the theological shallowness of the traditions they had inherited, welcomed the Calvinist revival and the shelves of ministers' studies began to fill with reprints of the classic works of Reformed doctrine and biblical exposition.

However, instead of providing Evangelicals with a secure foundation from which the challenges and questions raised by the modern situation might be explored in a positive and creative manner, the Calvinist revival tended to function as a bunker in the retreat from the forces of modernity. Attention was focused on the reformers' views of salvation and the nature of the church and little was heard of the radical nature of the Calvinist creed in relation to socio-political questions. Evangelical ministers who came to appreciate the spiritual depth of the Puritans as physicians of the human soul remained unaware of their commitment to the reform of society and its structures. The demand of the Puritan minister Thomas Case in 1641 that 'Reformation must be universal', the radical call to 'reform all places, all persons and callings' remained undiscovered and unappropriated by the majority of modern Calvinists. Consequently, the revival of Reformed theology too often led to a flight from the specific problems and dangers raised for faith by the contemporary situation and an avoidance of the task of relating belief to modern thought forms. In the language used throughout this book, the world-transformative nature of Calvinism went largely unrecognized and neglected.

However, there is evidence that Evangelicals are beginning to realize that historical Calvinism represented 'a fundamental alteration in Christian sensibility' in which flight from the problems of the social world to a privatized religion of personal devotion was replaced by 'the vision and practice of working to reform the social world in obedience to God' (Wolsterstorff:1983,11). The discovery of rich traditions of social theology to be found in the Dutch Reformed movement enables Calvinist Evangelicals to develop a Christian response to the problems of the modern world and this tradition, which anticipates the rejuvenation of the wastelands of modern society instead of their abandonment, may yet have much to contribute to the future of Evangelicalism.

A further voice in the modern Evangelical choir is that of the charismatic *House Church* constituency noted in the previous chapter. Like all new religious movements it has had to face the questions and problems which arise in the second and third generation, including issues related to organizational structure and the nurturing of established congregations. In 1988 almost a thousand House Church leaders met in conference in Sheffield and some observers saw this gathering as the first step in what sociologists would call the transition from sect to denomination. At the same time, voices within this group have asked searching questions concerning the social impact of charismatic religion. The Post Green Community at Poole in Dorset published a magazine entitled *Grassroots* which was designed to stimulate discussion on 'what it means for the church to be the people of God, a sign of celebration of life in Jesus Christ and a friend of the poor and oppressed'. This publication insisted that genuine renewal could never be restricted to the realm of the personal and spiritual, but must include the recovery of a prophetic and biblical concern for justice in the wider society. Another restorationist journal, *Tomorrow Today!*, included an article on Jesus' doctrine of the kingdom of God by Graham Cray, David Watson's successor as vicar of St Michael-Le-Belfrey, York. This was based on careful exegesis of biblical texts and insisted that the demands of the kingdom of God extend beyond Christ's reign over the lives of individuals who submit to him and requires both the challenging of dominant political ideologies and the announcement of good news to the economically poor and the socially powerless. The contents of this magazine indicated that some of the most prominent leaders in the Restorationist movement were developing a healthy self-criticism and were very aware of the limitations of the churches they led. This new, chastened mood was well expressed in the words of David Tomlinson, whose exposure to inner-city life in Brixton and Clapham led him to identify a question which is critical not merely for the future of the House Churches, but for the Evangelical movement as a whole:

> The New Churches in Britain are described as being among the fastest growing; their influence within the church as a whole is certainly increasing, but will they do more than refuel white, middle-class values? . . . Can we offer any real hope to our bleeding society? I think that is the question we must all answer (Tomlinson:1988,11).

A fifth voice, often unheard or ignored, is that of the *neo-Anabaptist* movement. After generations of neglect and vilification as the lunatic fringe of Protestantism, the heritage of the Anabaptists is increasingly welcomed and embraced by modern Christians who must discover the meaning and practice of discipleship in a secularized world. Historical research during the last thirty years has done much to clear away the mists of prejudice and misunderstanding which have long obscured the truth concerning the so-called Radical Reformation. At the same time, the problems and questions thrown up by secularization have predisposed many contemporary Christians to a sympathetic consideration of those who, at great cost, protested not merely at the corruption of the Roman Church, but the validity of the principles underlying the very existence of the *Corpus Christianum*. In an age in which the decline of Christendom has become obvious, the Anabaptist view that the whole enterprise represented a dreadful departure from apostolic Christianity, that, in fact, it was the outcome of the secularization of biblical religion, strikes a chord with those who must live in a world strewn with the ruins of past ecclesiastical power. Hendrik Kraemer described modern secularization as a kind of divine irony by means of which God calls the church back to its true nature; by this process the world has wrested from the church what the church should never have claimed, 'namely a usurpation of worldly power and a cramping authority over the intellectual and moral responsibility of man' (quoted in Verduin:1964,281). This was the view of the Anabaptists at the time of the Reformation and it is not surprising that a growing number of Evangelical Christians are responding positively to their insistence that the churches' correct relationship to the world involves neither assimilation nor domination, but a proper separation which makes possible the prophetic and missionary calling which is the fundamental task of the followers of Christ.

Interest in the Radical Reformation has also been stimulated by the emergence of Liberation Theology in Latin America. The liberationist critique of the Catholic Church and of traditional western theology, the establishing of 'base communities' within which an alternative view of life to that propagated by those who hold power is nurtured, and the insistence on the priority of revolutionary love within the Christian community, all this was clearly foreshadowed within the Anabaptist movement of the sixteenth century. One of the many terms of abuse flung at the men of the Radical Reformation was the word *kommunisten* because of their simple insistence that Christian discipleship had something to do with the teaching of Christ concerning riches and the example of the primitive church in redistributing wealth to meet the needs of the poor and suffering. Leonard Verduin has argued that if the western world had listened to the Anabaptists and allowed their teaching with respect to economics to influence public life, 'then Karl Marx would have had little . . . to write about' (Ibid:241).

In the event Marx had a great deal to write about. And after the experience at Lausanne, where they had learned from Third-World Christians whose theologizing was of necessity done in a revolutionary context, British Evangelicals began to give serious attention to Marx's critique of capitalist society. The 1970s were remarkable for the number of serious and informed studies of Marx and Marxism written by Evangelical authors. The trend was set when the Latin American theologian José Miguez Bonino was invited to deliver the first in a series of 'London Lectures in Contemporary Christianity' in 1974 under the chairmanship of John Stott. The lectures were published with the title *Christians and Marxists: The Mutual Challenge to Revolution*. The persistence of this quest for an adequate Christian social ethic which would take full account of Marx is demonstrated by the appearance of David Lyon's *Karl Marx: A Christian Appreciation of His Life and Thought* (1979) and Klaus Bockmuehl's *The Challenge of Marxism* (1980).

During the past decade some of the most searching critiques of conservative religion have come from the American radical activist, Jim Wallis. He has questioned the claim that the recent upsurge in 'born-again' religion represents a genuine revival in the context of secular society. Wallis has argued repeatedly that Evangelicalism has lost touch with its own spiritual and doctrinal roots and has allowed itself to be co-opted to provide religious legitimation for secular values. He describes western capitalism as 'the social rationalization of sheer selfishness', and says that the 'born-again phenomenon', instead of providing a challenge to 'one of the most self-centred cultures in history', has merely buttressed 'the consumer ethic of this society' (Wallis:1978,45). Wallis's radical critique is extremely disturbing to Evangelicals, not least because, while affirming the centrality of the call to conversion in the Christian message, he accuses his brethren of gutting the born-again experience of its moral and ethical content and, in the process, making it compatible with western civil religion.

Here themes first articulated by Anabaptist groups at the time of the Protestant Reformation are restated in a manner that gives them great contemporary relevance. For Wallis, Christian conversion always involves turning to the living God from idols and the enthroning of Christ as Lord requires the unmasking and dethroning of the false deities which usurp the Creator's rule in a fallen world. Wallis insists that it is in their response to concrete historical realities, to the evils of economic injustice and nuclear weapons, that professing Christians show whether or not they really belong to Christ. On the basis of this test the preachers of the New Religious Right are dismissed as 'Court Prophets' who merely provide an ideological justification for a thoroughly secular American way of life.

Wallis's books have been widely read and have provided an impetus toward the growth of a neo-Anabaptist perspective on socio-political issues. During a tour of Britain in 1986 his meetings attracted large numbers of young Christians. The secretary of the Scottish Baptist Union was present at a rally in Glasgow and reported that the large congregation consisted mainly of people under the age of thirty who were evidently 'deeply committed to Christ, alive to the immense needs of their world, and eager to be involved'. The worship in this meeting is described as 'the restrained celebration of those who would have felt it obscene to hold a party while so many in their world were crying in pain'. The Baptist leader came away from Wallis's preaching convinced that he had 'met a force to be reckoned with in our times – a force that by God's grace could turn our world upside down' (Barber:1986).

The voices we have identified so far strike obviously differ- ent notes, yet are capable of forming a single choir able to sing in harmony. *Mainline* Evangelicalism emphasizes the central- ity of conversion and the fundamental importance of spiritual unity in Christ; the *Anglicans* insist on commitment to the institutional church, decline the sectarian option and want to see Evangelicals involved both ecumenically and in the wider world; Evangelicals who have discovered the rich seam of *Reformed* theology warn against superficiality of belief or experience and bear witness to the glory and grace of God; *Charismatics* have recovered the early Evangelical focus on the Holy Spirit and insist that the Gospel sets the heart on fire and leads to wholeness; while the *Anabaptist* perspective emphasizes the costliness of discipleship and warns that following Jesus involves values that are counter-cultural in the modern world.

There is, however, a final voice which has sometimes seemed to strike a discordant note. It is that of the *Fundamentalists*. It is not clear whether this voice will further enrich the harmony of the Evangelical choir, or whether it is destined to sing solo. In fact it is difficult to find those who are willing to own this identity since, as we have seen, very few British Evangelicals have been willing to accept this term as a description of their position. However, we can identify Evangelicals who, in their definition of doctrine and in their approach to the modern world, clearly opt for a fundamentalist position. For example, the minister of London's Metropolitan Tabernacle, Peter Masters, brooks no compromise in the defence of conservative theology and regards involvement in ecumenism and talk of a dialogical approach to modern thought as tantamount to apostasy. His magazine, *Sword & Trowel*, carries articles with titles like 'The Crumbling of Evangelicalism' and 'Tracing the Rise of the New Evangelicalism: The Hastening Disaster'. Masters and his colleagues argue that faithfulness to biblical truth requires not only a separation from modernist theologians and churches, but a refusal to hold fellowship with Evangelicals who remain committed to what are called 'doctrinally mixed church associations'. The *Sword & Trowel* has endorsed the Fundamentalist taboo against alcohol, describing it as 'Satan's fermented river of false hope', and has mounted a persistent and highly sophisticated campaign against the theory of evolution. A writer in this journal articulated the policy of this group as follows: 'Others may seek to *modernize* the churches, but our God-given task is to *restore* primitive Christianity.'

Clearly, Fundamentalism of this kind, which insists on separatism and regards its understanding of the Christian faith as absolutely normative and non-negotiable, cannot easily play a part in the Evangelical coalition, let alone enter dialogue with the wider church concerning the task of mission at the close of the century. Yet the fact remains that Evangelicals who identify with the Fundamentalist concern to defend truth and worry about the real dangers involved in dialogue, could actually make a needed and valuable contribution within the movement at this critical time. No less a theologian than Nels Ferré, looking back on the battles fought in America in the 1920s, recognized that while the leaders of mainline Protestantism in America had gone over to 'the foe of a limited scientism and a shallow naturalism', the Fundamentalists 'held the main fortress'. Ferré suggested that if Fundamentalists could only 'get out from under the burden of an impossible literalism', they could make a valuable contribution to 'the making of the post-Protestant era of the Christian faith' (Glover:1954,246).

World-transformative Christianity and the task of mission in a post-modern culture

In recent years Evangelical theologians, drawing on the social sciences, have developed sophisticated models of cross-- cultural communication. Since the Lausanne Congress the question of the relationship of the Gospel to culture has been high on the Evangelical agenda and it has become axiomatic that Christian witness must be framed in ways that are culturally meaningful and sensitive. Missionaries are warned that the long and painful struggle to gain genuine understanding of a host culture cannot be regarded as something optional but is an absolute precondition for effective communication. Moreover, the battle with culture takes place on two separate fronts; he who struggles to relate the Gospel to an alien culture will soon discover that questions begin to arise concerning the degree to which his own pre-understanding of the Bible has been influenced, and possibly distorted, by the cultural lenses through which he has always read the text. Cross-cultural communication thus involves a dialectical process in which the missionary's questioning of his receptors evokes counter-questions concerning the congruence, or incompatibility, of the Gospel and modern, western culture.

Unfortunately, the persistence of the dichotomy between the 'Christian West' and the 'overseas mission field' has often prevented Evangelicals from recognizing the applicability of these missiological insights to the situation confronting the churches in Britain. Statements like that made by Keith Ward that, 'While most people are not actively connected with a religion, British culture is very strongly Christian in its basic ideals and values' (Ward:1986,150) are profoundly misleading and serve to delay discussion of the really critical questions concerning the Christian mission in contemporary society. This kind of analysis perpetuates the mindset of Christendom and, in so doing, prevents Christians from making the fundamental readjustments in thought and practice which are vital to the prosecution of the missionary task within the western world. In so far as British Evangelicals share Ward's illusion that their culture is 'strongly Christian', they will be condemned to live in a realm of fantasy while western society stumbles on, in Camus' words, 'without the aid of eternal values which, temporarily perhaps, are absent or distorted in contemporary Europe' (Camus:1975,7).

While there is undoubtedly a growing awareness among Evangelicals of the challenges which secularization poses to Christianity in western Europe, attitudes inherited from the era of Christendom still persist at the level of local churches and much Evangelical talk on the subject of evangelism betrays what Hoekendijk called 'a nervous feeling of insecurity . . . a flurried activity to save the remnants of a time now irrevocably past' (Hoekendijk:1950,163). The same writer identifies one of the key issues facing the churches of the West:

> In an unconscious way the national churches have become closed, because they related Christian community and nationality too exclusively, and in the West the churches have become class-churches, because they identified themselves too uncritically with one special group of society. It is nonsense to call these churches to evangelism, if we do not call them simultaneously to a radical revision of their life and a revolutionary change of their structure (Ibid:174).

It will be recalled that, more than a century ago, Edward Miall demanded just such radical changes in the belief that the identification of the churches with narrow class interests constituted an insuperable barrier to effective mission in an industrial society split apart by class divisions. Miall's pleas fell on deaf ears, partly because the argument for the establishment of religion retained plausibility at a time when the wider culture was still influenced, at least nominally, by Christian values. At the close of the twentieth century the gap between the Christian worldview and the value-system which operates at the heart of culture has become a chasm, with the result that attempts to gloss over the differences can hardly be credible and are likely to involve cynicism on the part of politicians or an unfaithfulness bordering on apostasy by Christians. C.E.M Joad reported the comment of a member of parliament during the Commons debate on the revised Prayer Book in 1928: 'For God's sake don't touch the Church of England: it is the only thing that stands between us and Christianity' (Joad:1937,209). The sociology of religion would suggest that this jibe contains truth which relates to institutional Christianity as a whole in a post-modern world. An established church will be likely to set limits to its prophetic critique of those who wield political power and, while the harm caused by such curbing of social criticism may be limited when church and state operate within the same value-system, the church's muted response to policies derived from political ideologies which clearly owe nothing to the Christian Gospel, can only further erode its credibility. Recent research has suggested that the 'irreversible breakdown of the situation in which Church and polity could be regarded as essentially coterminus' is the major problem facing the Church of England today. Colin Buchanan, former Bishop of Aston, has called for the loosening of the ties between the Church of England and a state which 'no longer acknowledges the God of the Old and New Testaments' and has said that at a time when 'Caesar is looking very Caesar-like', the people of God 'must surely be seen as God's people' (Buchanan:1989).

What is at stake here is the Christian response to the break-up of the sacral society of Christendom. Many Evangelicals lament this and understand evangelism as an effort to recover some of the ground lost in the process of secularization. But if the *Corpus Christianum* was itself the result of a historical development in which Christians lost sight of the distinction between 'the Old Testament theocracy and the New Testament church', and if the church's attempt 'to dominate society and culture' *invited* a secularist revolt (Clowney:1958,45), then secularization can be *welcomed* as a gracious opportunity for the churches to rediscover their true identity and missionary calling.

The focus of the preceding paragraphs has been on established churches, but Nonconformity also stands arraigned before the bar of history (to say nothing of Scripture), since, by its identification with the bourgeoisie, it made its own contribution to the process whereby Christianity surrendered to 'the social forces of national and economic life'. H. Richard Niebuhr described denominationalism as 'the accommodation of Christianity to the caste-system of human society' and warned that denominational religion was incapable of offering hope to a fragmented culture since it was 'no more able to stem the tide of disintegration in the world than it is able to set bounds to the process of disintegration within itself' (Niebuhr:1957,269).

In secular society the historic churches, including the Roman Catholic Church, are reduced to denominations, even though they may retain traditional privileges (the presence of Anglican bishops in the House of Lords, for instance) and perpetuate symbolic representations of past power and prestige. Bryan Wilson has described ecumenism as a defensive response of 'the Churches of the past' by means of which they endeavour, in the face of secularization, to reinforce 'their claims to status' (Robertson, ed.:1969,154). Thus, just as Hoekendijk criticizes certain types of evangelism as attempts to reverse the flow of history, so, for Wilson, the 'ritual dance of ecumenism' is a desperate ploy to shore up the crumbling walls of Christendom.

There is little doubt that a lingering nostalgia for the *Corpus Christianum* has played a part in the ecumenical movement. But Wilson may have overlooked a deeper and more radical change whereby churches of all denominations are compelled to engage in a process of critical reflection which is leading them toward an understanding of their nature and purpose which is close to the model of the Christian community found on the pages of the New Testament. Martin Marty has talked of the 'baptistification' of the churches, by which he means that the voluntarist style of Christianity, stressing personal response and demanding a distinctive pattern of life consonant with the profession of discipleship, is increasingly evident in *all* the churches. The 'church style' of the older denominations, Marty says, 'blended with culture so easily that many had no sense of having moved from anything to anything' and were left asking: What were the benefits of believing and belonging? (Marty:1983,34). Marty notes that Karl Barth and Jurgen Moltmann both raised serious theological challenges to the practice of infant baptism and he sees the Charismatic movement within the Catholic Church as a sign that members of that communion 'found something missing in the world they had known'. In fact, one can observe shifts of this kind taking place across the entire ecclesiastical landscape as the realities of a post-modern world expose the irrelevance of the structures of Christendom to the task of mission today. This underlines the conclusion that secularization brings positive benefits to all churches by compelling them to make a fundamental re-evaluation of their purpose and calling in the world, so providing an opportunity, or a *kairos*, for the rediscovery of their true nature.

If the present situation compels the historic churches to recognize the removal of their privileges and the loss of their traditional status in western society as positive gains, Evangelicalism could have a vital role within a Christianity which, chastened by secularization, discovers its missionary calling within the modern world. David Bosch has said that ever since Constantine's victory at the battle of Milvian Bridge in AD 312, the western church has been compromised to privilege in one form or another. To this day, he says, the church in the West has still not been liberated from 'the guilt of privilege' and the hardest, and most urgent, lesson it must learn if it is to fulfil its mission in the conditions which prevail at the close of the twentieth century, is 'how to become again what it originally was and was always supposed to be: the church without privileges, the church of the catacombs rather than the halls of fame and power and wealth' (Bosch:1987,15). Evangelicalism, with its traditional stress on the centrality of the cross of Jesus Christ and the necessity of personal response to the Gospel, should be in a position to assist the emergence of the modern church-in-mission. However, as this study has shown, Evangelicalism has itself tasted the beguiling pleasures of power and privilege and is unlikely to fulfil its potential in the post-modern era without a frank and humble recognition of its own compromises and illicit alliances.

While the reformation of the church is one indispensable condition for the fulfilment of the Christian mission in the modern world, the creation of a credible Christian apologetic is another. Christians must ask themselves not only 'What must we be?' but 'What must we say?' While secularization compels the church to make a critical examination of its structures, it also raises inescapable questions concerning the form and content of its message. Karl Heim, who devoted most of his life to the attempt to construct a meaningful apologetic for Christianity in the modern world, believed that the future of the church depended upon her ability to engage in dialogue with the world and to 'answer the questions which it puts to her'. He suggested that in-house theological disputes pale into nothingness 'so long as no answer has been given to the question whether the whole thing is not, after all, as Feuerbach supposed, only a projection'. What is at stake, Heim argued, is the significance and justifiability 'of all religious seeking and striving' (Heim:1953:31). More recently, Lesslie Newbigin has argued that the critical issue facing the church today is whether the West can be converted and he demands that, instead of trying to understand the Gospel from the perspective of our culture, we begin to ask what it might mean 'to understand our culture from the point of view of the gospel' (Newbigin: 1987,5).

Implicit within Newbigin's question is the problem of the normative basis of theology or, as the title of one of Helmut Thielicke's books asks, *How Modern Should Theology Be?* Many sociological analyses identify this as the crux of the problem which modernity poses for religious belief, the so-called cruel dilemma which offers theology the choice of relevance at the price of jettisoning historic Christian truth-claims, or faithfulness to those claims at the cost of the exclusion of religious discourse from the discussion of the central concerns of modern culture. The fact that contemporary theologies can be classified according to just such a twofold schema, as 'modernist/Liberal' or 'traditionalist/Conservative' appears to confirm this sociological insight. Since it is now clear that the preservation of traditional beliefs by a form of cultural quarantine is as damaging to the true interests of religion as is its assimilation to secularism, the need for a synthesis which would make possible theological relevance without compromise, and Christian faithfulness which does not involve retreat from the real world, is absolutely critical. Neither theologies 'which attempt to maintain their Christian identity only by ignoring their context in the modern world', nor those 'which simply accept the modern world in a rationalistic and positivistic way' can resolve this dilemma (Bauckham:1987,140).

Our concern here is with the Evangelical response to this situation and it is worth recalling the Lausanne Covenant's affirmation of the need for churches to be 'closely related to their culture'. In a finely balanced statement the Covenant acknowledged that *all* human cultures are both 'rich in beauty and goodness' *and* imperfect and capable of the demonic (Douglas J.D., ed.:1975,6). When applied to the West, this affirmation provides the basis for a response to modern culture which is balanced and critical, a response, that is, which affirms all that is good in pluralistic societies, while maintaining a critical perspective derived from an understanding of human existence and purpose which is itself independent of modern culture.

In a way, as Thielicke has pointed out, the categories traditional/modern involve a false dichotomy since any serious, contemporary theology will endeavour to harmonize its statements with the truth derived from historical and scientific study. Even the most conservative of Evangelicals attempt to validate their theology by reference to scientific criteria. For Thielicke the central issue is not whether theology should be modern in this sense, since Christ desires not merely the conscience, the emotions, the anxieties, of those he calls, but their reason, knowledge and consciousness as well. Thielicke insists that the scientist and the historian must run to meet Christ with minds that are wide awake and intact and must never be asked to repress the truth discovered by means of honest, critical investigation (Thielicke:1970,15–16). However, modernity 'becomes a curse' when we permit ourselves 'the privilege of deciding what can be truth for us', when it leads us to 'welcome only the God who fulfills the conditions which we must impose in order to be able to accept him as God' (Ibid:17). Such 'reductive' theology abandons the possibility of a critical perspective toward western culture since, as Peter Berger has said, it assumes that contemporary people stand on a 'cognitive pinnacle' from which they can analyze and overcome the shortcomings of the rest of humankind (Berger:1979,119).

The existentialist philosopher Karl Jaspers once said that in the extremity of our age, the best chance of deliverance may lie with the churches if, with renewed earnestness, they would 'repeat the eternal challenge to man: to be changed in his foundations – and in conjunction with everyday life, with all that men do and think'. The human situation, Jaspers said, demands a rebirth of man (Bockmuehl:1980,163–4). There are many indications at the close of the twentieth century that a long era is coming to a close. The theme of spiritual rebirth which Jaspers believed to be so important today, lies at the very centre of the Evangelical understanding of the Gospel; it dominated the preaching of the eighteenth-century evangelists, while for Victorian Evangelicals the call to conversion 'was the content of the gospel' (Bebbington:1983,19). And yet, as Evangelicalism changed over time, so its understanding of the nature and consequences of conversion was modified in all kinds of ways with the result that the biblical promise of the New Humanity was watered down to an offer of personal peace and happiness. Gutted of its scriptural content, conversion was reduced to an experience which required no radical break with the values of a secular culture; indeed, conversion became a purely private affair bearing so little relevance to the public sphere that a widespread resurgence of born-again religion could occur without posing the remotest threat to a society whose prosperity is built on the justification of greed and whose security rests upon a willingness to commit genocide and turn God's earth into an uninhabitable wasteland. Evangelicalism, no less than Liberalism and Catholicism, ceased to have *critical* contact with western culture and became party to the veneration of modern forms of the sacred – the nation-state, the ideology of 'guaranteed security' and, above all, the cult of Mammon, which the Bible frankly calls idols. Conversion became a means of personal, psychological release from the historical situation and those who experienced it were left, in Aquaviva's words, 'totally integrated with the society, religiously degraded, reduced to one dimension' (Aquaviva: 1979,194). The resultant peaceful co-existence between the church in the West and the culture of the Enlightenment has led Newbigin to describe European Christianity as 'an advanced case of syncretism' (Newbigin:1983,23).

The contemporary situation reveals extraordinary opportunities for Evangelicals. The emptiness of modern life, the loss of hope in the societies of East and West, the massive threats to human survival posed by the uncontrolled developments of a technological culture, and the increasing difficulties in defending a genuinely scientific perspective amid the myriad forms of contemporary irrationality, all confirm Jaspers' diagnosis and amplify his call for a rebirth of humankind. Yet if the analysis of Evangelicalism in this book is anywhere near correct, a movement which has allowed its central theme to be domesticated and privatized, leaving it unable to recognize the extent to which it has become ensnared in the worship of the idols which dominate western culture, is itself in need of radical conversion. Evangelicals must heed the criticisms of the enemies of middle-class religion whom they have too often ignored or dismissed as 'infidels'. Those who stand outside the church have sometimes spoken with extraordinary clarity of the tragic failure of believers to live and act consistently with the Gospel. Evangelicals can learn from what has been called *protest* atheism in the works of people like Marx, Nietzsche and Camus. Thus, Thielicke acknowledges that Nietzsche's arrogance in opposing God is not guilty hubris, but 'a prejudice induced by the empirical phenomenon of Christianity, its institutions, its theology, and its behaviour'. Nietzsche stands, he says, not for apostasy, but for *reaction against apostasy*, and his critique is not to be rejected but 'received and taken to heart' (Thielicke:1968,251–2).

I have mentioned the testimony of missionaries who find themselves undergoing a disconcerting experience in which their own concepts and values are challenged and trans-formed. Like Jonah in Nineveh, or Peter in the household of the Gentile Cornelius, she who crosses cultural boundaries to preach for the conversion of others is likely to find her sum-mons echoing back to search and revolutionize her own life. If Evangelicalism begins to take seriously the missionary task which confronts it within the western world, it will itself be converted in the process. Such a change will be neither painless nor cheap. In place of comfortable and undemanding religion, genuine conversion will involve the confession of Jesus as LORD and a determination to live in the light of the values of the kingdom of God revealed in his life, death and resurrec-tion. The alternative, and it is a path Evangelicalism might be persuaded to take, is the refusal of a missionary stance toward modern culture, the continued privatization of religion and the acceptance of an ideological role in justifying things as they are. In that event, Evangelicalism will have betrayed those who founded the tradition two centuries ago and will have shown that it no longer shares the divine concern for those who are sickened and wearied by life in the Far Country because, like the elder brother in Jesus' parable, it has yielded to a spirit of slavery and become blind to its own need of grace.

Select Bibliography

The books and articles included in this list have been restricted to those actually cited in the text.

Andrews, Stuart	1969	'John Wesley and the Age of Reason' *History Today*, XIX:25–32
Aquaviva, Sabino	1979	*The Decline of the Sacred In Industrial Society* Oxford: Blackwell
Balleine, G.R.	1908	*A History of the Evangelical Party in the Church of England* London: Longmans, Green
Barr, James	1978	*Fundamentalism* London: SCM Press
	1984	*Escaping from Fundamentalism* London: SCM Press
Bauckham, Richard	1987	*Moltmann: Messianic Theology in the Making* Basingstoke: Marshall Pickering
Bebbington, David	1983	'The Gospel in the Nineteenth Century' *Vox Evangelica*, 13:19–28
Barber, Peter	1986	'Scene Around' *Scottish Baptist*, August 10
Berger, Peter	1977	*The Heretical Imperative: Contemporary Possibilities for Religious Affirmation* New York: Anchor/Doubleday
	1979	'Religion and the American Future' in *The Third Century: America as a Post-Industrial Society* Seymour Lipset (ed.) Stanford: Hoover Institution Press

Best, Geoffrey   1970   'Evangelicalism and the Victorians'
                             in Anthony Symondson (ed.) *The
                             Victorian Crisis of Faith* London:
                             SPCK

Bockmuehl, Klaas 1980 *The Challenge of Marxism – A Chris-
                             tian Response* Leicester: Inter-
                             Varsity Press

Booth, General   1890   *In Darkest England And The Way Out*
                             London: Salvation Army

Bosch, David J.   1987   'Vision for Mission' *International
                             Review of Mission*, LXXVI: 8–15

Bonino, José   1976   *Christians and Marxists: The Mutual
Miguez   Challenge to Revolution* (1974 London
                             Lectures in Contemporary Christian-
                             ity) London: Hodder & Stoughton

Brierley, Peter   1982   *UK Christian Handbook: 1983 Edition*
(ed)   London: Evangelical Alliance

Briggs, John &   1973   *Victorian Nonconformity* London:
Sellars, Ian (eds)   Edwin Arnold

Brown, Callum G. 1981 'Religion and the Development of
                             an Urban Society: Glasgow 1780–
                             1914' Unpublished PhD Thesis,
                             University of Glasgow

Brown, Ford K.   1961   *Fathers of the Victorians: The Age of
                             Wilberforce* Cambridge: Cambridge
                             University Press

Bruce, Steve   1980   'The Student Christian Movement
                             and the Inter-Varsity Fellowship: A
                             Sociological Study of Two Student
                             Movements' Unpublished PhD
                             Thesis, University of Stirling

                     1982a 'The SCM: A Nineteenth-Century
                             Movement and Its Vicissitudes' *In-
                             ternational Journal of Sociology and
                             Social Policy*, 12:67–82

                     1982b 'Born Again: Conversion, Crusades
                             and Brainwashing' *Scottish Journal
                             of Religious Studies*, 3:107–23

Buchanan Colin   1989   *The Guardian*, January 7

Butler, Pierce   1937   'Irvingism as an Analogue of the Oxford Movement' *Church History*, 6:101–12

Calver, Clive   1988   *The Independent*, April 20

Cameron, N.M. de S.   1982   'Dean Burgon and the Bible: An Eminent Victorian and the Problem of Inspiration' *Themelios*, 7/2:16–20

Camus, Albert   1971   *The Rebel* Harmondsworth: Penguin Books

Carey, George   1988   'Parties in the Church of England' *Theology*, XCI:266–73

Carson, H.M.   1969   *Farewell To Anglicanism* Worthing: Henry Walter

Carson, John T.   1966   *Frazer of Tain* Glasgow: United Committee of Christian Organizations

Chadwick, Owen   1966   *The Victorian Church – Part I* London: Adam & Charles Black

Chalmers, Thomas   1820   *The Application of Christianity to the Commercial and Ordinary Affairs of Life* Glasgow: Chalmers & Collins

Clowney, Edward P.   1958   'Secularism and the Christian Mission' *Westminster Theological Journal*, 21:19–57

Cockshut, A.O.J.   1959   *Anglican Attitudes: A Study of Victorian Religious Controversies* London: Collins

Collier, Richard   1968   *The General Next To God: The Story of William Booth and the Salvation Army* Glasgow: Fontana/Collins

Cox, Jeffrey   1982   *The English Churches in a Secular Society: Lambeth, 1870–1930* Oxford: Oxford University Press

Cunningham, Valentine 1975   *Everywhere Spoken Against: Dissent in the Victorian Novel* Oxford: Clarendon Press

Dallimore, Arnold   1970   *George Whitefield: The Life and Times of the Great Evangelist of the*

		Eighteenth-Century Revival Vol.1 London: Banner of Truth
Denney, James	1891	'Biblical Inspiration' *British Weekly*, IX:354
	1903	*The Atonement and the Modern Mind* London: Hodder & Stoughton
Dickens, Charles	n.d.	'Two Views of a Cheap Theatre' in *The Uncommercial Traveller* [First published 1876] London: Chapman and Hall
Douglas, J.D. (ed.)	1975	*Let The Earth Hear His Voice* Official Reference Volume: Papers and Responses at International Congress on World Evangelization in Lausanne. Minneapolis: Worldwide Publications
Dunbabin, J.D.P.	1974	*Rural Discontent in Nineteenth-Century Britain* London: Faber & Faber
Edwards, David L.	1988	*Essentials: A liberal-evangelical dialogue* London: Hodder & Stoughton
Edwards, Jonathan	1834	*The Works of Jonathan Edwards* Vol. 2 London: Westley and A.H. Davis
Eliot, George	1855	'Evangelical Teaching: Dr Cumming' *The Westminster Review* VIII: 436–62
	1973	*Scenes From Clerical Life* [First published 1858] Harmondsworth: Penguin
	1986	*Middlemarch* [First published 1874] Oxford: Clarendon Press
Evangelical Alliance	1968a	*On The Other Side: The Report of the Evangelical Alliance's Commission on Evangelism* London: Scripture Union
	1968b	*Background To The Task* London: Scripture Union
Foster, John	1867	*Essays, in a series of letters* London: Bell & Daldy
Fountain, D.G.	1966	*E.J. Poole-Connor, 1872–1962:*

Contender for the Faith Worthing: Henry Walter

Frank, Douglas   1986   *Less Than Conquerors: How Evangelicals Entered the Twentieth Century* Grand Rapids: Eerdmans

Fullerton, W.Y.   1934   *C.H. Spurgeon, A Biography* London: Williams and Norgate

Fundamentals, The n.d.   (12 vols. published 1910–15) Chicago: Testimony Publishing Co.

Gilbert, Alan D.   1976   *Religion and Society in Industrial England: Church, Chapel and Social Change, 1740–1914* London: Longman

Gladstone, W.E.   1879   'The Evangelical Movement: Its Parentage, Progress and Issue' *The British Quarterly Review* LXX: 1–26

Glover, Willis B.   1954   *Evangelical Nonconformists and Higher Criticism in the Nineteenth Century* London: The Independent Press

Gosse, Edmund   1986   *Father and Son: A Study of Two Temperaments* [First published 1907] Harmondsworth: Penguin

Graham, W. Fred   1978   *The Constructive Revolutionary: John Calvin and his Socio-Economic Impact* Atlanta: John Knox Press

Gray, Arthur B.   1921   *Cambridge Revisited* Cambridge: Heffer

Griffiths, Brian   1982   *Morality and the Market Place* London: Hodder & Stoughton
                     1984   *The Creation of Wealth* London: Hodder & Stoughton

Griffiths, Terry   1988   'Can These Bones Live?' *Mainstream,* 28:1–3

Guinness,   1950   *Sacrifice: A Challenge to Christian Youth* 4th ed. London: Inter-Varsity Fellowship
Howard W.

Guthrie, Thomas   1851   *The City: Its Sins and Its Sorrows* Edinburgh: Adam and Charles Black

Haldane, Robert 1834 *The Evidence and Authority of Divine Revelation* 2 vols, 2nd. ed. London: Hamilton Adams

Harries, John 1930 *G. Campbell Morgan: The Man and His Ministry* New York: Fleming H. Revell

Hastings, Adrian 1986 *A History of British Christianity: 1920–1984* London: Collins

Heim, Karl 1953a *Christian Faith and Natural Science* London: SCM Press

1953b *The Transformation of the Scientific Worldview* London: SCM Press

Hoekendijk, Hans J. 1950 'The Call To Conversion' *International Review of Mission*, 39:162–75

Hopkinson, William H. 1983 'Changing Emphases in Self-Identity Among Evangelicals in the Church of England: 1960–1980' Unpublished MPhil Thesis, University of Nottingham

Howden, J. Russell n.d. *Evangelicalism: Essays By Members of the Fellowship of Evangelical Churchmen* London: Thynne and Co.

Inglis, K.S. 1963 *Churches and the Working Class in Victorian England* London: Routledge and Kegan Paul

Jay, Elisabeth 1979 *The Religion of the Heart: Anglican Evangelicalism and the Nineteenth-Century Novel* Oxford: Clarendon Press

1983 *The Evangelical And Oxford Movements* Cambridge: Cambridge University Press

Joad, C.E.M. 1937 *The Testament of Joad* London: Faber & Faber

Kent, John 1978 *Holding The Fort: Studies in Victorian Revivalism* London: Epworth Press

Kiernan, V. 1952 'Evangelicalism and the French Revolution' *Past and Present*, 1:44–57

Kingsley, Charles 1983 *Alton Locke* [First published 1850] Oxford: Oxford University Press

Lenton, Tim 1988 'End of Evangelicalism?' *Church of England Newspaper* May 27

Livingstone, David N. 1987 *Darwin's Forgotten Defenders: The Encounter Between Evangelical Theology and Evolutionary Thought* Edinburgh: Scottish Academic Press

Lloyd-Jones, D.M. 1952 *Maintaining The Evangelical Faith Today* London: Inter-Varsity Fellowship

1964 *The Weapons of Our Warfare* Glasgow: Pickering & Inglis

Lyon, David 1979 *Karl Marx: A Christian Appreciation of His Life and Thought* Tring: Lion Publishing

Magnusson, Norris 1977 *Salvation In The Slums: Evangelical Social Work, 1865–1920* (ATLA Monograph, Series 10) Metuchen, NJ.: The Scarecrow Press

Marsden, George 1980 *Fundamentalism and American Culture: The Shaping of Twentieth-Century Evangelicalism, 1870–1925* Oxford: Oxford University Press

Marty, Martin 1983 'Baptistification Takes Over' *Christianity Today* September 2: 33–6

Masterman, N. (ed.) .1900 *Chalmers on Charity* London: Constable

McLeod, Hugh 1974 *Class and Religion in the Late Victorian City* London: Croom Helm

1984 *Religion and the Working Class in Nineteenth-Century Britain* London: MacMillan

Mearns, Andrew 1970 *The Bitter Cry of Outcast London* [First published 1883] Edited Andrew Wohl, Leicester: Leicester University Press

Meek, Donald E. 1987 'Evangelical Missionaries in the

		Early Nineteenth-Century Highlands' *Scottish Studies*, 28: 1–34
	n.d.	'The Land Question Answered from the Bible: The Development of a Highland Theology of Liberation' Unpublished Paper
Meredith, Albert R.	1973	'The Social and Political Views of Charles Haddon Spurgeon, 1834–1892' Unpublished PhD Thesis, Michigan State University
Miall, Edward	1849	*The British Churches in Relation To The British People* London: Arthur Hall Virtue
Moule, Handley C.G.	1965	*Charles Simeon* London: Inter-Varsity Press
Murray, Iain	1971	*The Puritan Hope: A Study in Revival and The Interpretation of Prophecy* London: Banner of Truth
	1982	*David Martyn Lloyd-Jones – The First Forty Years* Edinburgh: Banner of Truth
Newbigin, Lesslie	1983	*The Other Side of 1984* Geneva: WCC
	1987	'Can the West be Converted?' *International Bulletin of Missionary Research*, 11/1: 2–7
Newsome, David	1966	*The Parting of Friends* London: John Murray
Nicoll, W. Robertson	1890	*The British Weekly* September 12
Niebuhr, H. Richard	1957	*The Social Sources of Denominationalism* Cleveland: Meridan books
Oliphant, Mrs	1862	*The Life of Edward Irving* 2 vols. London: Hurst and Blackett
Orr, James	n.d.	*The Christian View of God and the World as Centring in the Incarnation* (Kerr Lectures, 1891) 10th ed. Edinburgh: Andrew Elliot
Packer, J.I.	1958	*Fundamentalism and the Word of God* London: Inter-Varsity Press

Padilla, C. René (ed.) — 1976 — *The New Face of Evangelicalism* London: Hodder & Stoughton

Plumb, J.H. — 1963 — *England in the Eighteenth Century* Harmondsworth: Penguin Books

Pollock, J.C. — 1953 — *A Cambridge Movement* London: John Murray

1978 — *Wilberforce* Berkhampsted: Lion Publishing

Poole-Connor, E.J. — 1966 — *Evangelicalism in England* 2nd ed. Worthing: Henry Walter

Punch — 1844 — 'Exeter Hall Pets' vi: 210

1856 — 'Invitation to the May Meeting' XXX:209

Rennie, Ian — 1962 — 'Evangelicalism and English Public Life 1823–1850' Unpublished PhD Thesis, University of Toronto

Robertson, Roland (ed.) — 1969 — *Sociology of Religion – Selected Readings* Harmondsworth: Penguin Books

Rogers, T. Guy (ed.) — 1923 — *Liberal Evangelicalism* 3rd ed. London: Hodder & Stoughton

Rosman, Doreen M. — 1978 — 'Evangelicals and Culture in England, 1790–1833' Unpublished PhD Thesis, University of Keele

Runcie, Robert — 1988 — Unpublished Address to NEAC3, available from Church of England Evangelical Council, Chippenham

Ryle, J.C. — 1952 — *Holiness* London: James Clarke

Saward, Michael — 1995 — 'Behind the Plenaries' in Charles Yeats (ed.), *Has Keele Failed? Reform in the Church of England* London: Hodder & Stoughton

Schaeffer, Francis — 1968a — *Escape From Reason* London: Inter-Varsity Press

1968b — *The God Who Is There: Speaking Historic Christianity into the Twentieth Century* London: Hodder & Stoughton

1970 — *The Church At The End Of The Twentieth Century* London: The Norfolk Press

Scotland, Nigel   1986   'Francis Close: "Cheltenham's Protestant Patriarch" ' in James Thrower (ed.), *Essays In Religious Studies for Andrew Walls* Aberdeen: Department of Religious Studies, Aberdeen University

Scougal, Henry   1976   *The Life of God in the Soul of Man* (First published, 1677) Minneapolis: Dimension Books

Semmel, Bernard   1974   *The Methodist Revolution* London: Heinemann

Sider, Ronald J. 1977   *Rich Christians in an Age of Hunger* Downers Grove: Inter-Varsity Press

Smyth, Charles   1943   'The Evangelical Movement in Perspective' *Cambridge Historical Journal* VII/3:160–74

Stott, John (ed.) 1977a *Obeying Christ in a Changing World, vol. 1 The Lord Christ* Glasgow: Collins

                  1977b *What is an Evangelical?* London: Church Pastoral Aid Society

                  1988   *NEAC3: A Report on the National Evangelical Anglican Celebration* Chippenham: Church of England Evangelical Council

Strong,   1899   *Christ in Creation and Ethical Monism*
Augustus H.   Philadelphia: Griffith & Rowland Press

                  1962   *Systematic Theology* (First published, 1907) London: Pickering & Inglis

Thielicke, Helmut 1970   *How Modern Should Theology Be?* Glasgow: Collins/Fontana

Thurman, Joyce V. 1982   *New Wineskins: A Study of the House Church Movement* Frankfurt am Main/Bern: Verlag Peter Lang

Tomlinson, David 1988   'Unity and Society' *Tomorrow Today!* October(2): 10–11

Triggs, Kathy   1986   *The Stars and the Stillness: A Portrait of George MacDonald:* Cambridge: Lutterworth Press

Troeltsch, E.   1931   *The Social Teaching of the Christian Churches* 2 vols. New York: Harper & Brothers

Van den Berg, J.   1956   *Constrained by Jesus' Love* Kampen: J.V. Kok

Verduin, Leonard   1964   *The Reformers and Their Stepchildren* Exeter: Paternoster Press

Walker, Andrew   1985   *Restoring the Kingdom: The Radical Christianity of the House Church Movement* London: Hodder & Stoughton

Wallis, Jim   1978   'Conversion' *Sojourners*, May

                       1982   *The Call To Conversion* Tring: Lion Publishing

Ward, Keith   1986   *The Turn of the Tide: Christian Belief in Britain Today* London: BBC Publications

Ward, W.R.   1972   *Religion and Society in England, 1790–1850* London: B.T. Batsford

Weber, Max   1985   *The Protestant Ethic and the Spirit of Capitalism* London: Unwin Paperbacks

Wickham, E.R.   1957   *Church and People in an Industrial City* London: Lutterworth Press

Wilson, Bryan   1976   *Contemporary Transformations of Religion* Clarendon Press: Oxford

Wohl, Anthony S.   1970   *The Bitter Cry of Outcast London* with
(ed.)   leading articles from the *Pall Mall Gazette* of October 1883, etc. Leicester: Leicester University Press

Wolterstorff,   1983   *Until Justice and Peace Embrace* Grand Rapids: Eerdmans
Nicholas

Wood,   1960   *The Inextinguishable Blaze* London:
A. Skevington   Paternoster Press

Yeo, Eileen   1981   'Christianity in Chartist Struggle, 1838–1842' *Past and Present*, 91: 109–39

Zabriskie,   1940   'Charles Simeon: Anglican
Alexander   Evangelical' *Church History*, 9: 101–19

Name Index

Subject Index